Make it in Denim

Make it in Denim

Hazel Todhunter

B T BATSFORD LTD LONDON

First published 1977

Illustrations by Hazel Todhunter

ISBN 0 7134 0663 1 (hardback)
ISBN 0 7134 0662 3 (paperback)

Filmset in 10 on 11 pt. Photina by
Servis Filmsetting Ltd, Manchester
Printed in Great Britain by
The Anchor Press Ltd, Tiptree, Essex

for the publishers B T Batsford Ltd
4 Fitzhardinge Street, London W1H 0AH

CONTENTS

DENIM – ITS HISTORY

Denim is the fashion phenomenon of recent years but it has a long history. Two hundred years ago a brave new world had been discovered. It was a time of enterprise and of enterprising young men, out to make their fortunes. In France a strong, durable fabric had been developed for the sails of the clipper ships that were being built to trade with the Americas. It came from Nîmes. It was not long before Americans produced it for themselves – after all they produced the cotton it was made from, and they had a growing textile industry.

It was strong, durable, cheap and white. Settlers going west took it with them, they even covered their wagons with it. They used it for overalls and dungarees, but the colour was not very practical – so they dyed it blue, using a dye extracted from an indigenous plant – indigo.

In California, men were trying to make fortunes digging gold out of the hills. Another enterprising young man – Levi Strauss – made waist overalls for them. At first they were made of sailcloth, but later from *Tissus de Nîme*, now called denim. They were in great demand. The size did not matter too much – the wearer simply jumped into the nearest horse trough and his levis shrunk to fit. Jeans, as we know them, had arrived, complete with rivets, which were originally used to repair the pockets that the miners were forever pulling off.

By 1930 jeans were cheap, casual wear and were being mass produced. They were so common that American schools complained at the amount of damage the rivets were doing to school furniture. During the Second World War jeans were standard government issue. They first arrived in Britain with the G.I.s – general issue!

At the end of the war came a boom in education and the creation of a new class – students. (They had been known before but not in such numbers.) Their common bond was poverty – they sought cheap, hard-wearing clothes – and found them in government surplus. In 1945 people literally queued outside shops to buy jeans. There were not many horse troughs around so jeans were shrunk by sitting in the bath. Faded jeans were a status symbol, indicating that one could afford to roam abroad or laze in the sun during the holidays – not supplement one's income by working. Inevitably came do-it-yourself bleaching – and very odd were some of the results. Rivets were augmented by studs. Denim had arrived.

DENIM – THE FABRIC

Technically, denim is a stout, twill weave, cotton fabric. From a practical point of view that means it is ideal for beginners. It does not slip and slide about, or stretch out of shape. Nor does it fray unduly. You will find denim in the fabric departments of large stores – and in many smaller shops. It comes in 90 cm (36 in) width; in several colours and textures – including brushed; also with woven and printed patterns. So please do not think purely in terms of good old blue denim.

Denim has a coloured warp and white weft – the twill weave means that it comes out two sided – one side light, the other side dark. Always check that you are buying denim – not sailcloth, which is the same both sides. Sailcloth or any other fabric will not make up in the same way and you will be disappointed with the results.

I refer to denim by weight. Heavyweight denim is the type used for good quality jeans, very stiff when it is new. Lightweight is that used for shirts. Medium as its name implies is somewhere inbetween and is usually made into dresses. If a garment needs interlining buy the same weight interlining as the denim.

TOOLS

Keep all your tools together in a suitable container. A work basket or work box is luxurious, but not essential; a cutlery tray also keeps the items separate. I use a bread basket, but a shoe box or a biscuit tin is quite sufficient and can always be decorated – see printing section. Store the article on which you are working in a clean pillow-case or polythene bag. (Do remember to keep polythene bags away from children since they can lead to suffocation.)

Scissors
Sharp scissors are essential. Blunt scissors fray the fabric, making it difficult to work with. In this case even the good workman can blame poor tools. You will need two pairs of scissors, a large cutting out pair and a small pointed pair for cutting threads and trimming fabric. (A cork on the points of the scissors keeps them sharp and avoids the danger of cut or scratched fingers.) Keep a pair of household scissors for cutting paper – as this ruins sharp scissors.

Tape measure
Used to check measurements and in marking out fabric. Choose a strong tape measure that will not stretch.

Chalk
This, too, is used for marking out fabric. Tailor's chalk is best as it has a sharp edge for drawing. Keep chalk away from work, preferably in an envelope or small polythene bag as it tends to crumble over everything.

Needles
Keep a selection of needles, in their packets or in a needle case so that they are easily found.

Pins
Use long glass-headed pins for heavyweight denim and long dressmaker's pins for other weights. Keep them in a tin, small box or screw-top jar. A piece of polyurethane foam stuck to the top provides a pin cushion. (A small piece of chalk or a few grains of rice kept with the pins prevents them rusting.)

Tacking cotton
You can still buy tacking thread – but you might as well use odd reels of cotton for tacking. Choose a colour that shows up well. (Red is the traditional colour.)

Thimble
This may seem old-fashioned, but it saves sore fingers, especially when sewing heavyweight denim. Make sure it fits properly – or it will rub. (If you really cannot use a thimble, sticking plaster helps to protect finger tips.)

Dressmaker's carbon
This is used to transfer designs to the denim; ordinary carbon paper is not suitable as it smudges too easily. To use it, pin the denim to a board, right side up. Cut a paper mask which leaves the design area exposed. Place this on the denim. Place the carbon paper on top, carbon (shiny) side down, then place the design on top and pin in place. Carefully go over the lines of the design with a ball-point pen or pencil. (A fibre-tip pen will not do.) Lift one corner and check that the impression is clear enough; if not, go over the design again. Lift off the carbon, mask and design. (Masking the denim prevents carbon rubbing off where you rest your hands.)

Iron
An iron and a clean cloth are essential for pressing. A steam iron is ideal, and an ironing board makes pressing seams easier.

Sewing machine
This is very useful, but not essential. Denim will take big, bold hand stitching, which is almost as quickly worked as machine stitching. Take good care of your sewing machine. Oil it regularly and remove any build up of fluff. Choose the right needle for the thread and weight of fabric you are using. Always check the machine tension before use.

Fabric adhesive
A rubber based adhesive, such as Copydex, which is specially made for fabric, is best. Always apply it sparingly, with a spent match or cocktail stick, as it marks fabric if it comes through to the right side. Spread a small amount of adhesive on both surfaces to be joined. Wait for it to become tacky – then press surfaces together. Be warned, they will stick as soon as they touch. If you do not allow the adhesive to dry a little the pressure of your fingers will force it through to the right side of the denim.

Knife and straight edge
These are used for cutting templates and trimming card. A small craft knife is best, and cheapest. Use it with a metal ruler, or ruler with a metal inset. An ordinary ruler will suffice, but it is easier to cut into it (or your fingers!). Always keep your fingers behind the knife blade; *never* in front.

BASIC SEWING

Shrinking fabric

Denim is a cotton fabric and can shrink dramatically. It is worth the time and effort to pre-shrink the fabric – otherwise the garment might not fit after the first wash. Wash fabric in hot water (60°C/140°F) for the maximum wash, or leave to soak in very hot water until the water cools enough to wash by hand. Spin or wring. Press whilst fabric is damp, until dry.

Measurements

All the sizes in this book have been worked out in metric and imperial, so that in many cases the measurements given are not absolutely accurate conversions. Use either metric or imperial as desired.

Cutting out

The problem with cutting out fabric is finding enough space – it is much easier if you can spread the fabric out. A table is adequate for small things, but for garments a clean floor is the best, if not the most convenient, place. I compromise, and mark out fabric on the table but cut out on the carpet. It has advantages; pins stuck into the carpet hold the denim in place and it is easier on the knees as you crawl around – but beware of stray pins. Before cutting out make sure that you understand the instructions. (Try them out using newspaper if necessary.) Make sure the denim is pre-shrunk. To mark a line parallel to the selvedge (the firm woven edge of the fabric), use the blunt end of a pin or needle to pull out a thread.

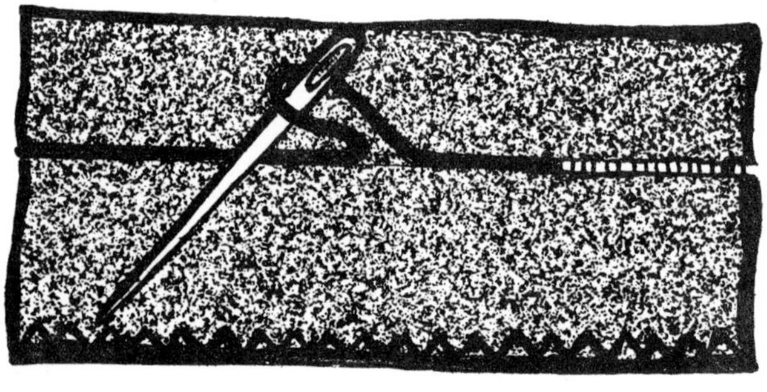

Threads across the fabric are difficult to remove. Lines are best marked with tailor's chalk and a tape measure or ruler. Use large scissors to cut the fabric. Since denim, especially heavyweight denim, can be hard to cut, wrap cotton-wool or knitting wool round the handles of the scissors to protect the hands. To avoid confusion, use tailor's chalk to write the name on the back of each piece as it is cut out.

Tacking

Careful tacking makes the rest of the sewing easier. Use cotton that shows up clearly. Make a knot at the end of the thread and stitch close to the edge of the hem or seam. Use large running stitches, they can be up to 2.5 cm (1 in) long. To remove, cut thread and pull out using the blunt end of a needle or pin.

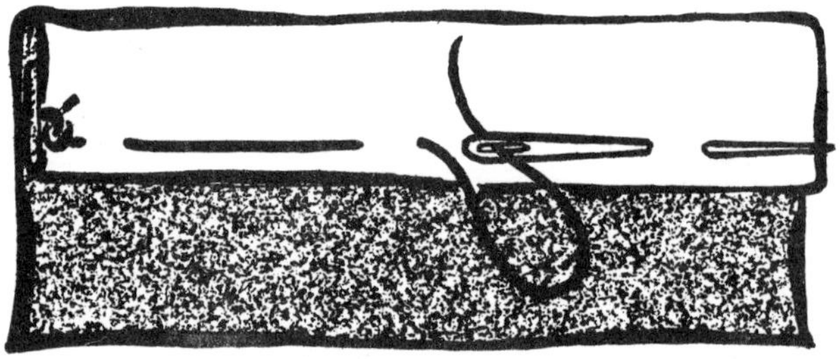

Seams

Seams should be strongly sewn and the same width along their length. Poorly sewn seams will part company long before the denim wears out. Make sure that all thread ends are securely fastened. It is better to fasten on thread with several small stitches rather than with a knot – for knots always pull out. Pull machine threads to the back of fabric and knot together. To sew seams, use machine stitching, stab stitch or back stitch. Stab stitch is quicker than back stitch but not so strong. A compromise is to work stab stitch with a back stitch every few stitches for strength.

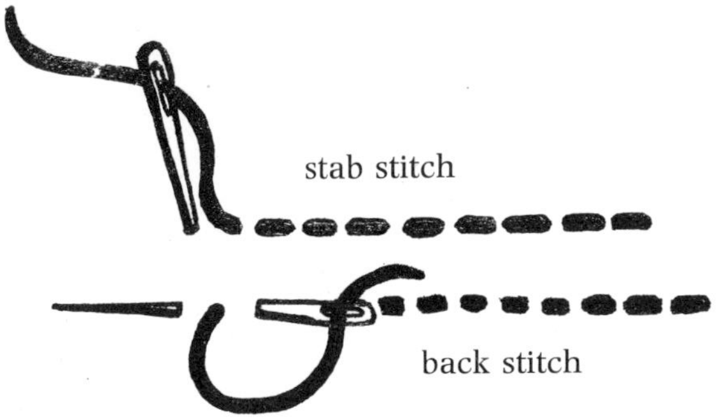

Flat seam Make sure that you have the correct sides together. Then pin and tack carefully, using a piece of card as a guide to keep the width even. Normally this seam is 1.5 cm ($\frac{5}{8}$ in) wide. Remove tacking and press well before continuing.

Run and fell seam This seam is used where both sides of the fabric show, or where a seam ends in a hem. Make flat seam with one edge of fabric 0.5 cm ($\frac{1}{4}$ in) below the other.

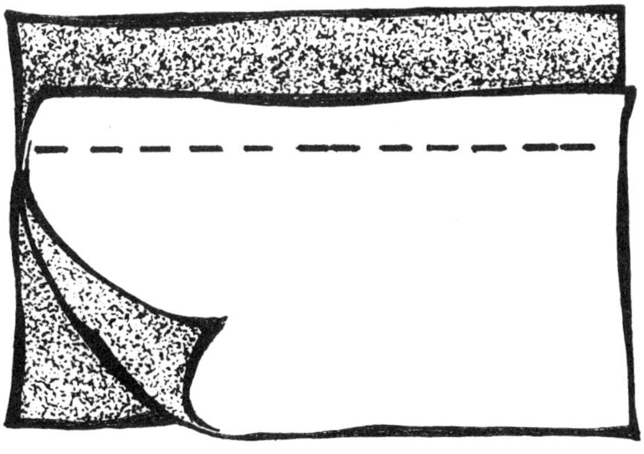

Fold in raw edge on wider turning and press.

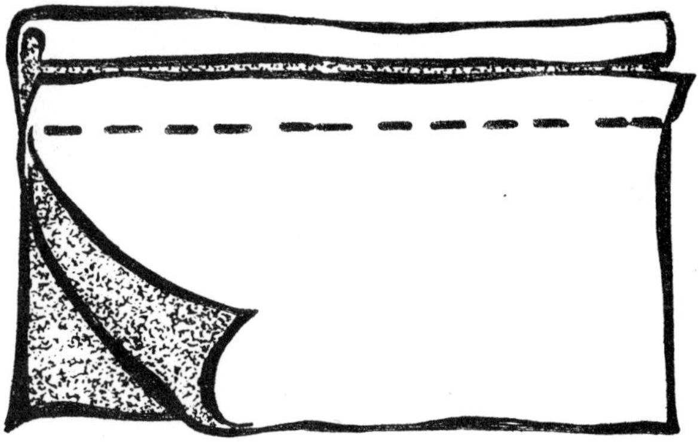

Fold edge over and tack into place. The fold can then be topstitched or hemmed. Remove tacking and press well.

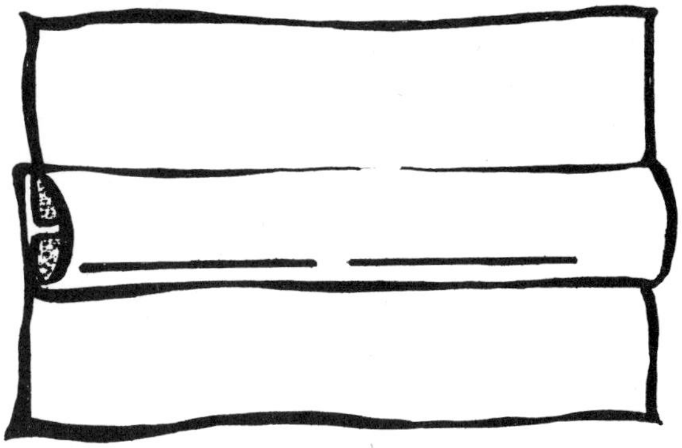

Hems

Hems need careful preparation. Fold hems with the right side of the fabric towards you. Turn down 1 cm ($\frac{3}{8}$ in) and hold it with the thumb and forefinger of one hand, whilst creasing the fold between the thumb and forefinger of the other hand. Make the second fold of the hem in the same way, this time making it the width given

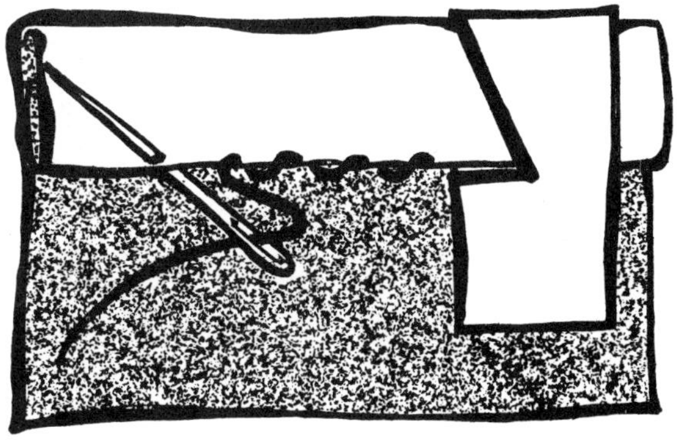

in the instructions. Tack and press. Make sure that the hem is of an even width; a small piece of cardboard cut to the width of the hem can be a great help. Topstitch or hem into place. Unless otherwise stated all hems are turned to the front.

Gathering
This is used to fit a full sleeve into a cuff, or a skirt into a band or yoke. Thread a needle with sufficient cotton to sew the edge to be gathered in one go. Fasten thread firmly, about 1 cm ($\frac{3}{8}$ in) from edge, and work one row of running stitch. Leave end unfastened. In the same way work a second row of running stitch just above the first row. Use loose ends to carefully pull up gathers. If you are using a machine, set it at its longest

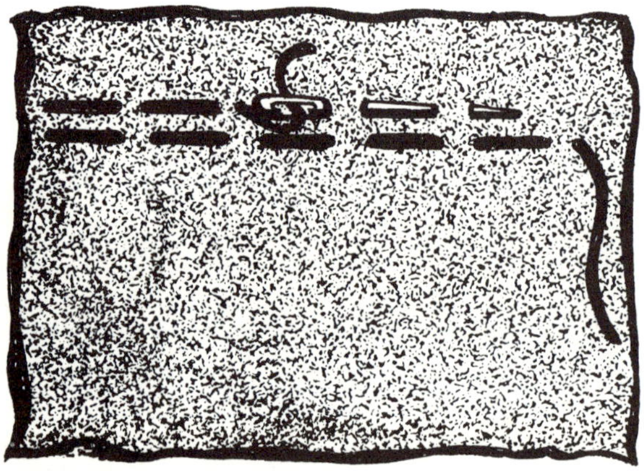

stitch. You will find it much easier to pull up the underneath thread, which comes from the bobbin. Use two threads; they make the gathers more even, and if one thread breaks it is not necessary to start again. To attach the gathered edge to the band, place the edge of the band to the edge of the gathers, right sides together, and pin at intervals. Adjust gathers to fit. Put in more pins to secure gathers, then tack carefully. Sew using a flat seam and a small stitch so that each gather is held in place. Remove tacking and press the band; avoid pressing the gathers.

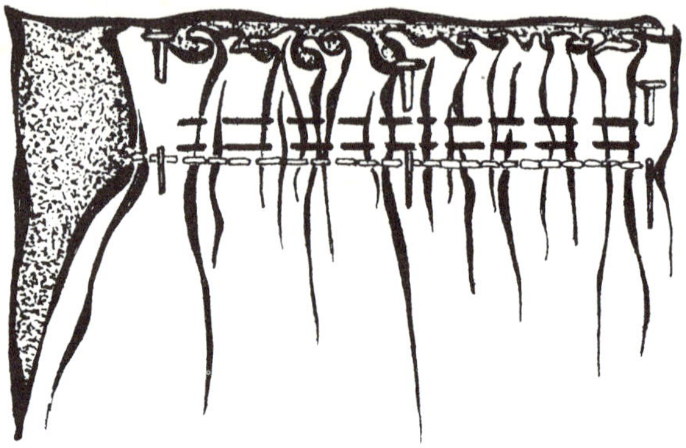

Oversewing
This is used to join two neatened edges, or for eyelets.

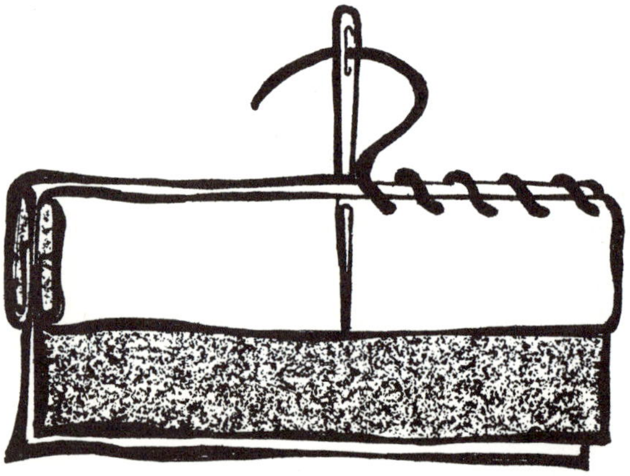

Pressing
Pressing is essential for really good, professional looking results. Keep the ironing board out and the iron hot so you do not miss out this vital step. Use a hot iron (set for cotton) and a clean, damp cloth over the fabric – or use a steam iron. Press fabric until it is dry. If pressing a lot of material, e.g. after shrinking, I find it easier to iron on a table: there is less heaving and hauling of fabric. Put several thicknesses of blanket on the table to protect the surface.

BASIC TECHNIQUES

Bands
These are used to cover raw edges. Make bands with the wrong side of the fabric towards you. Turn down 1 cm ($\frac{3}{8}$ in) and hold it with the thumb and forefinger of one hand, whilst creasing the fold between the thumb and forefinger of the other hand. Make fold on other edge in the same way. Tack and press.

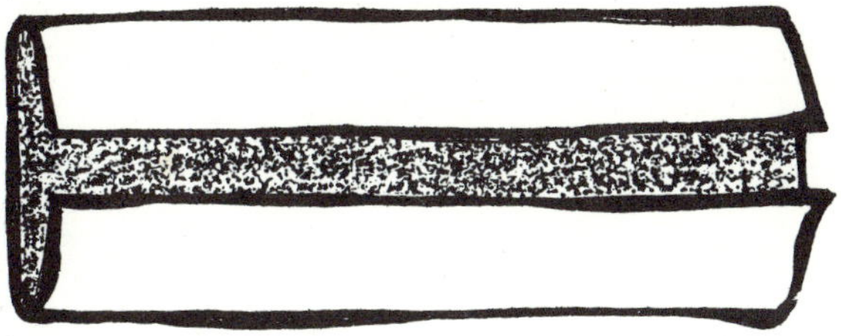

Eyelets
You can buy metal or plastic eyelets in many of the larger shops. They come with instructions for use. A punch is used to cut a hole and a second punch is used to flatten the edges of the eyelet – or you can get 'pliers' which combine both functions. Personally, I dislike both sorts. Since the fabric is cut it tends to fray – and the eyelets fall out; this process is hastened by any strain placed on the eyelet. If you want to use commercial eyelets you should use sufficient strength to really flatten the eyelets so that they grip the fabric.

A much better way is to mark the position of the eyelet with a pin. Then move the pin around to make a small hole. Enlarge this hole by pushing through a knitting needle. Buttonhole or oversew the edges.

To make a larger eyelet, mark the position, then make two small cuts. Fold edges to wrong side and trim if necessary. Oversew or buttonhole edges closely.

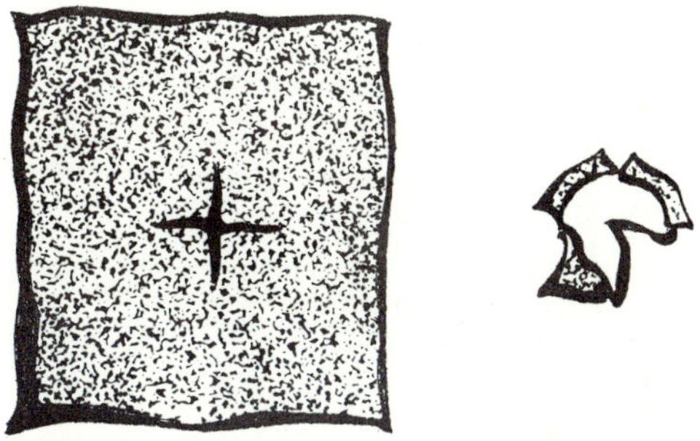

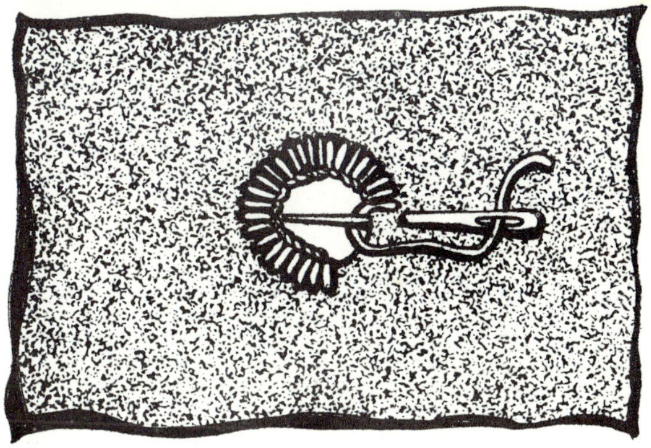

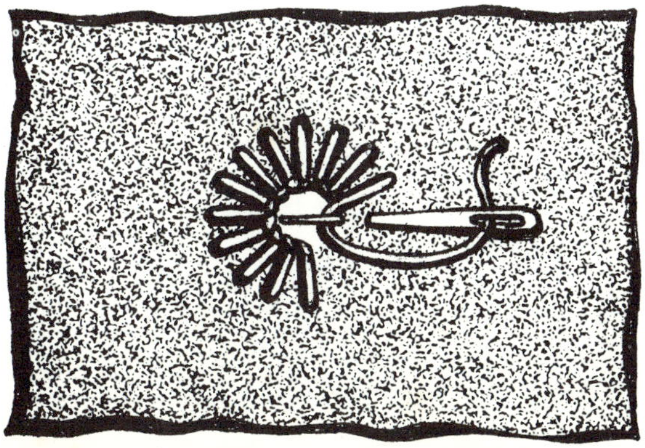

Mitred corners
This is done wherever two hems of equal width meet at a right angle.

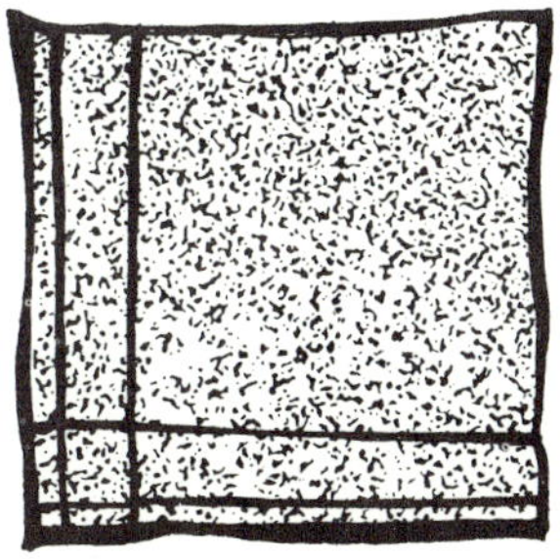

a) Turn in and crease both the adjacent hems. Do not tack or press – you are only marking the corner. Open out and trim off the corner as shown.

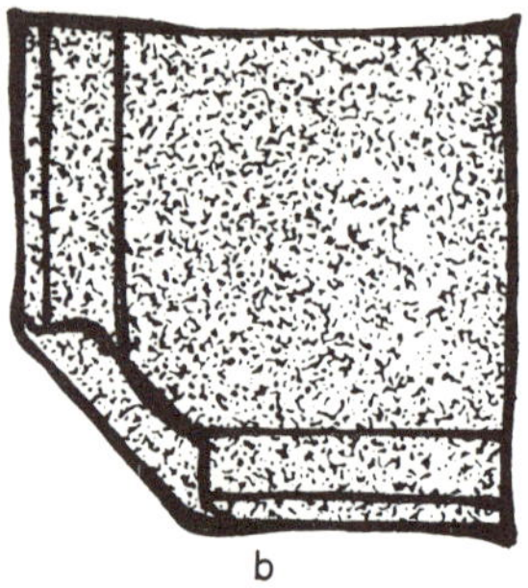

b

b) Turn corner in and crease into place.

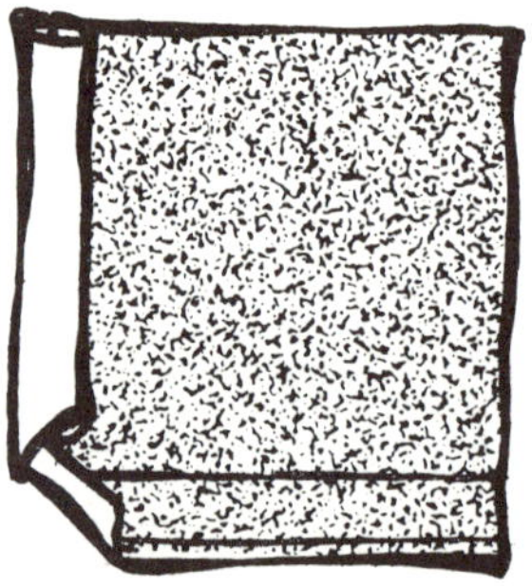

c

c) Turn in one hem. Tack and press.

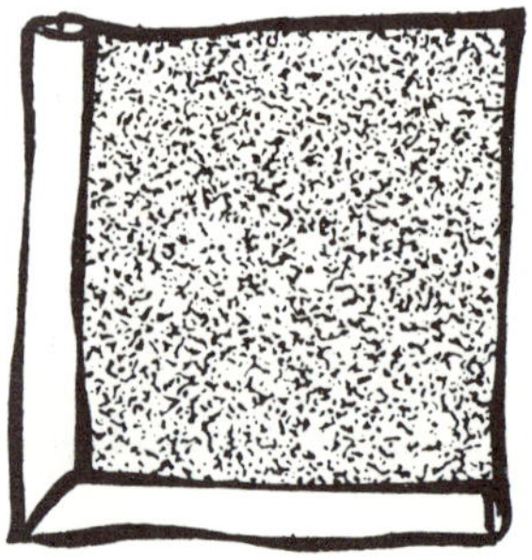

d

d) Turn in second hem. Tack and press. Hem or topstitch into place.

Press studs

These can be used to fasten bags, pouches and clothes. Modern press studs of clear plastic do not look as clumsy as the older metal ones, and there is no chance of them rusting.

Press the top of the stud into the bottom, then mark the position of the bottom of the stud. Fold over the flap and mark the position of the top of the stud by pushing a pin or needle through the tiny hole of the centre of the press stud. Oversew both parts of the stud into place.

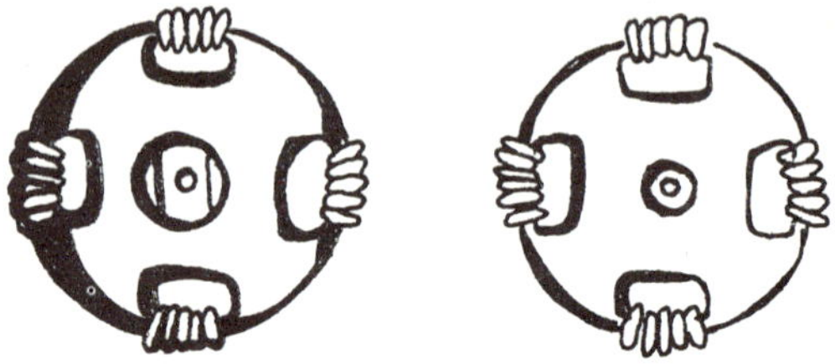

Rouleau

This is used to make handles, belts or ties. Fold the strip in half with right sides of the denim together. Join with a 1 cm ($\frac{3}{8}$ in) flat seam. Use a pencil, ball-point pen or knitting needle to turn fabric through to the right side. Turn in ends and oversew to neaten.

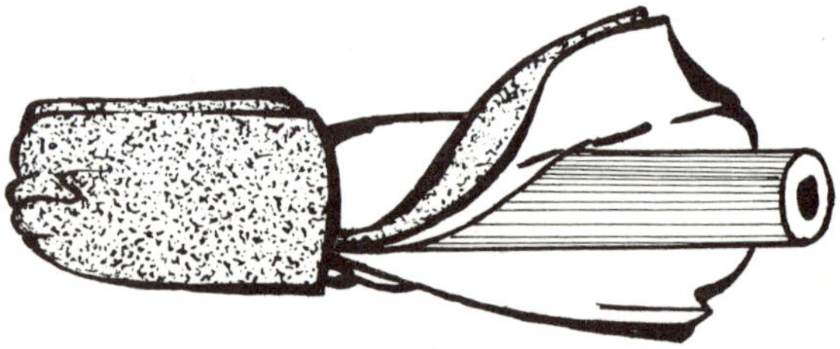

Another method is to turn 1 cm ($\frac{3}{8}$ in) to the wrong side of fabric, as if making a band. Then fold strip in half to enclose raw edges. Oversew edges, or topstitch close to edge. Turn in ends and oversew.

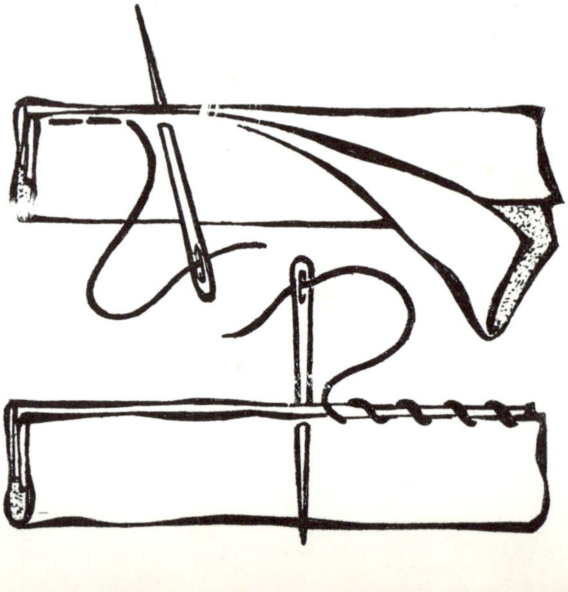

Touch fastening

This is a useful way of fastening bags or pouches. Touch fastenings, such as *Velcro*, consist of two tapes, one of which has a fluffy surface, the other of which has tiny hooks. Where they touch they fasten. Mark position of fastening. Then cut a short length from each tape. Pin into position then oversew into place. It works best if the fluffy piece is sewn to the bag and the hooked piece is sewn to the flap. Be careful that the stitches do not show on the right side of the flap.

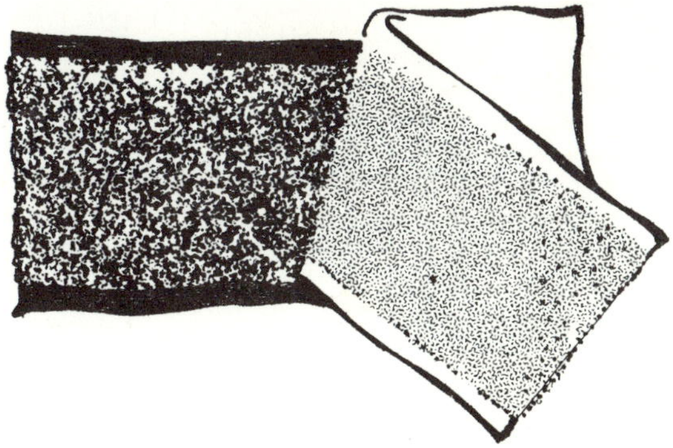

BASIC EMBROIDERY

Whipped running stitch; also shows how to work running stitch

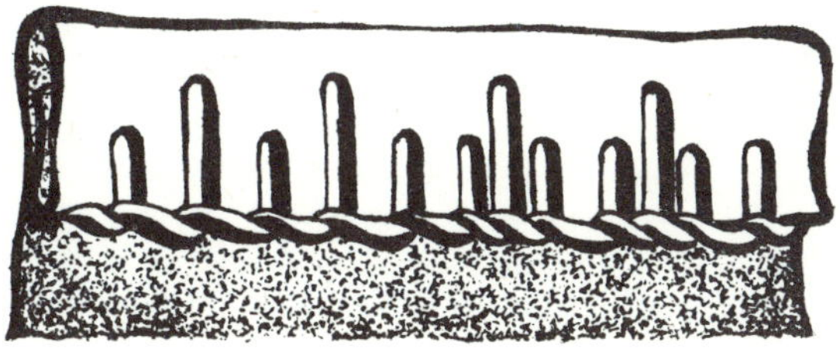

Laced running stitch

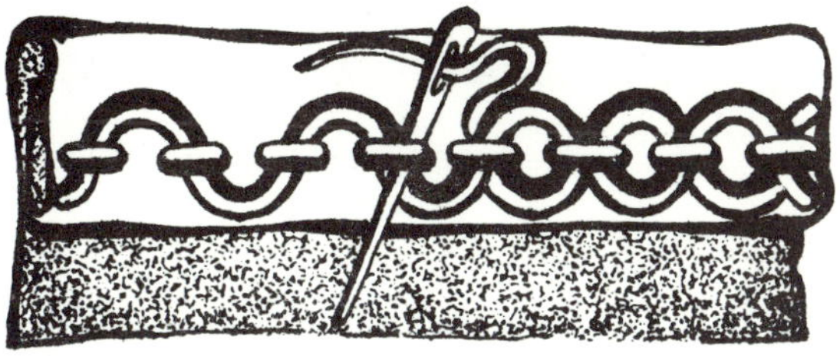

Threaded running stitch, using two different coloured threads

Pekinese stitch; this uses a row of back stitch – not running stitch

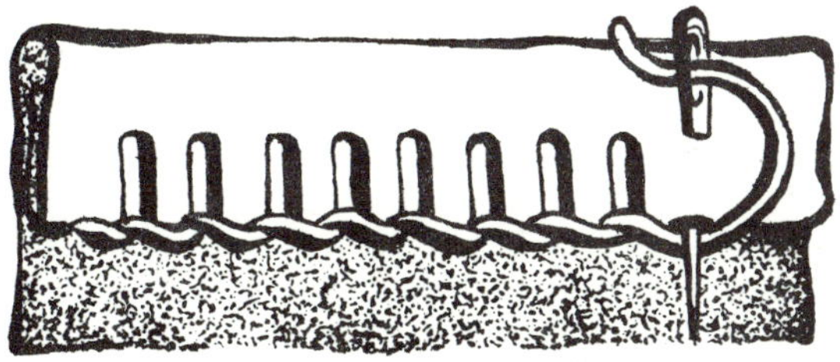

Threaded running stitch, using one thread laced through two rows of running stitch

Blanket or buttonhole stitch

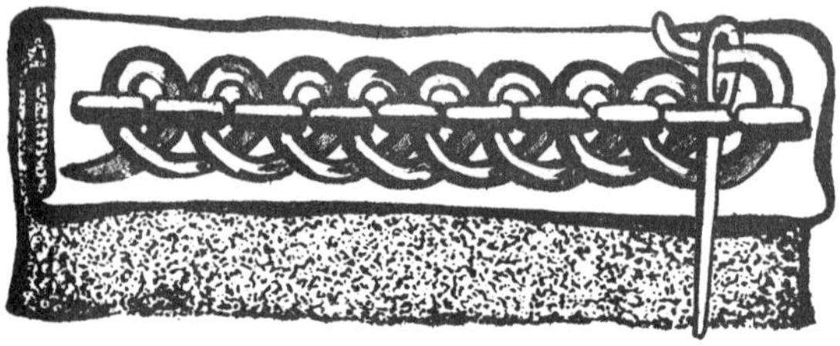

Blanket or buttonhole stitch; alternate long and short stitches grouped in various ways

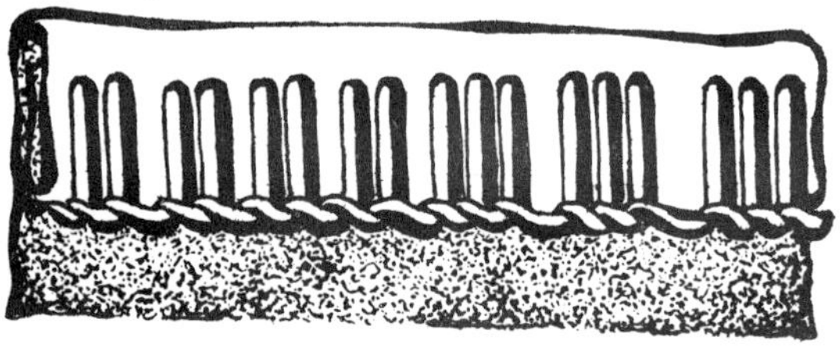

Blanket or buttonhole stitch, long stitches in groups of two or three

Blanket or buttonhole stitch, stitches slanted to leave triangular spaces

Fly stitch; used to secure a hem

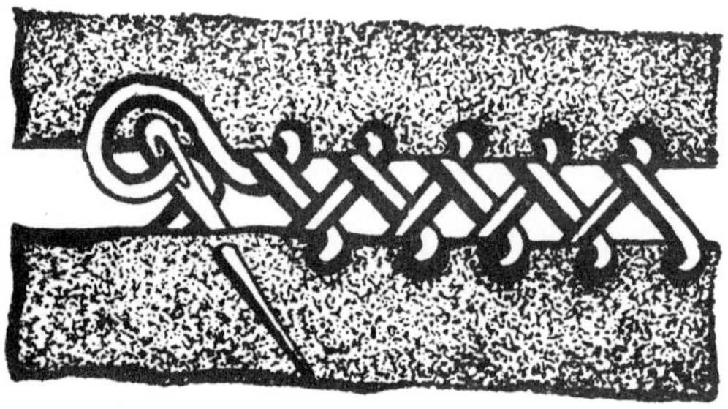

Faggoting

Buttonhole insertion; could also be grouped in twos

Laced buttonhole stitch

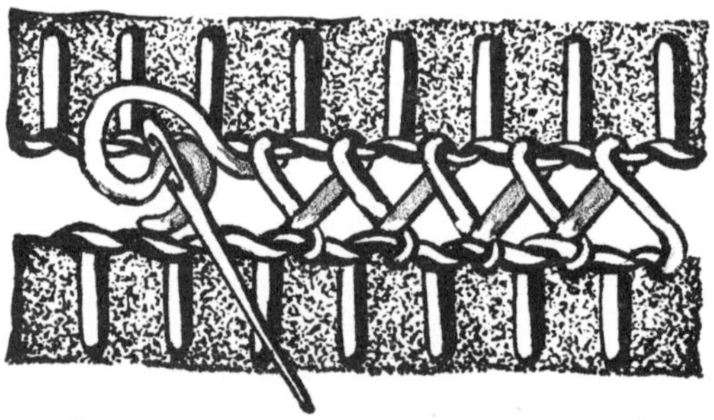

Buttonhole stitch with twisted lacing

Chain stitch, also separate chain stitch, often known as lazy daisy

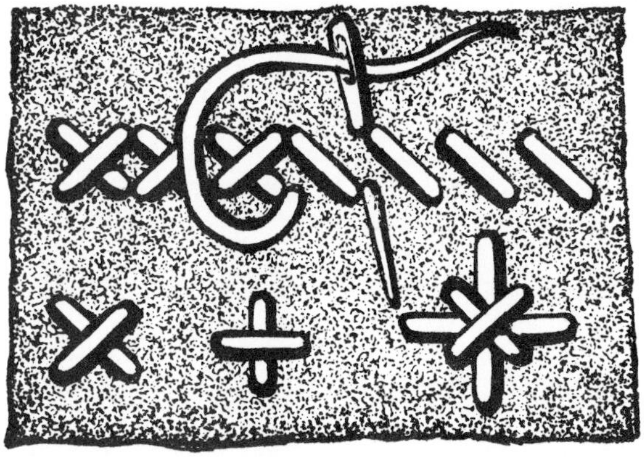

Cross stitch, work; it is best to work one stroke of each cross all along the line and then return, adding a second stroke; separate cross stitches can be built up into stars

Fly stitch; single fly stitches grouped

WASHING

Denim is a cotton fabric and washes well, but care has to be taken with some forms of decoration; do not ruin them by careless washing. Do not wash anything containing card, and remove dowel rods before washing.

Plain denim
Always wash denim separately, for the colour normally runs. This is particularly important with new denim. Machine wash in hot water 60°C/140°F) for the maximum time, or handwash in hot water. Spin or wring. Iron whilst still slightly damp. If denim has dried, use a clean, damp cloth or a steam iron.

Painted or printed denim
Although painted or printed garments can be machine washed they benefit from special care. Wash in hand hot water (40°C/104°F) and soap flakes. Keep garment as flat as possible and avoid squeezing or wringing. Detergent can cause some paints to fade. Rinse thoroughly and drip dry away from direct heat, as this can crack the paint. Hanging up such clothes after each wearing prolongs their life.

Denim with decorative seams
Articles with decorated seams can be machine washed as for ordinary denim, but are best washed in hand-hot water and dripped dry, as the washing machine or spin dryer can strain or rip the insertion stitches. Also the cooler water prevents too much colour running into the embroidery. Beware of catching stitching with the point of the iron.

Embroidered denim
Denim loses less colour at lower temperatures. Machine or hand washing embroidered articles in hand-hot water (40°C/104°F) prevents colour running into the embroidery. Spin or wring. Iron whilst still damp, covering the embroidery with a cloth to avoid snagging the stitches with the point of the iron.

Padded appliqué or quilted denim
The quilting fabric used is normally Terylene and will not stand very hot water without matting and losing some of its bounce. So machine wash in hand-hot water (40°C/104°F) medium or minimum wash – or hand wash. Spin or wring. Avoid over-pressing such work or it will flatten and lose its springiness.

Metal decoration on denim
Any garment with metal decoration, such as metal eyelets of metal rings should not be left to soak. Dry such articles as quickly as possible. Avoid catching the point of the iron in rings or eyelets. If there is a lot of decoration cover it with a clean cloth before ironing.

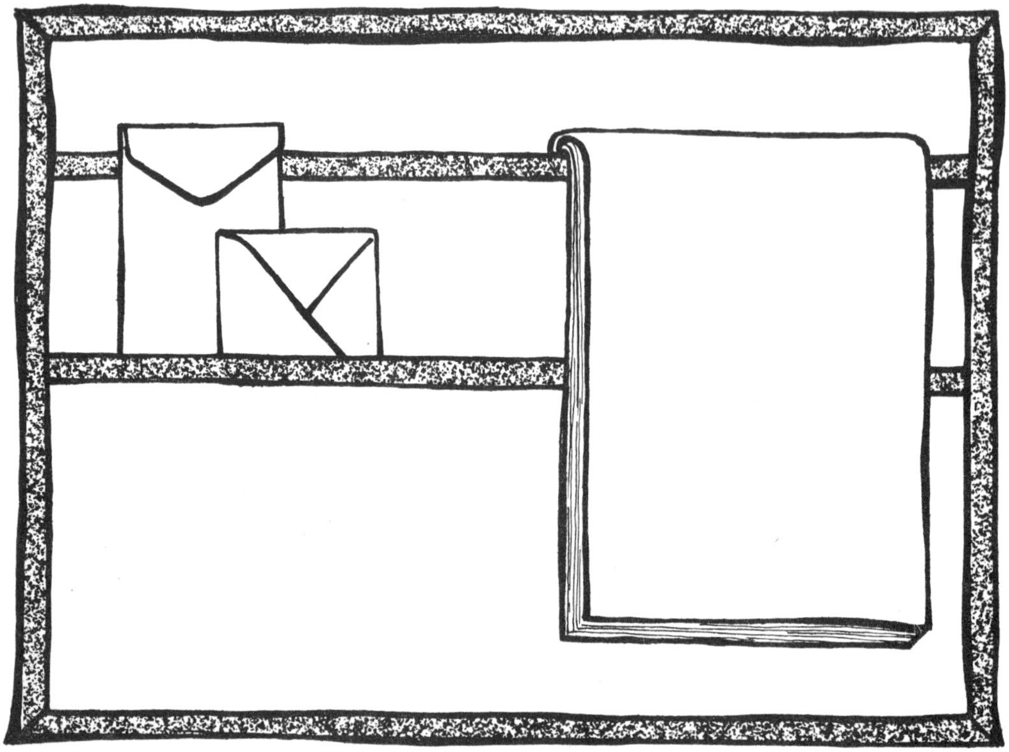

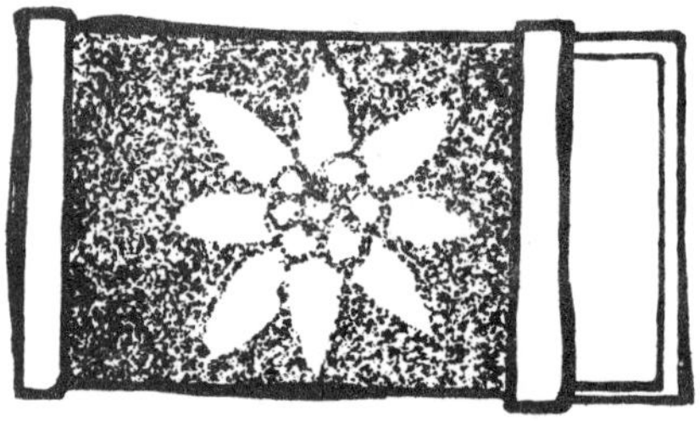

Writing case (open and shut), pencil holder, bits-and-bobs box

BLEACHING

Bleaching is very easy to do, but limited in its uses because it weakens the fabric. Bleached denim is not strong enough for making garments, but can be added to them in the form of pockets or appliqué. It is most effective on indigo dyed denim.

Equipment

a piece of board slightly bigger than the design
a piece of polythene sheet the same size
newspaper
chalk
drawing-pins
flour
saucer
household bleach
a child's paint brush
a sponge in a saucer of water

Technique

Spread several layers of newspaper on the board to soak up surplus bleach. Place denim, dark side up, over this and pin in place. Sketch in design using chalk. Place polythene over denim and cut out piece covering design to mask against drips. Pin in place. In the saucer, mix flour to a thick paste with water. Using the wrong end of the paint brush, apply paste in blobs to the centre of the design. Leave to harden. The paste resists the action of the bleach and leaves a dark centre to the motif. Pour bleach into a small container which is unlikely to tip over. Use paint brush to paint in the petals and then paint over the paste. Use sponge to mop up any spills or splashes. Allow to dry. Paint on bleach again if necessary. Do not leave the bleach where a child can find it, pour it away or tip it back into the bottle. Allow to dry. Scrape off as much paste as possible, then wash thoroughly in detergent. Dry and press.

Pencil holder

Materials Empty plastic bottle with straight sides; piece of denim long enough to go round bottle, plus 5 cm (2 in) and 15 cm (6 in) deep; adhesive.
Cutting out Cut two 2.5 cm (1 in) strips from a long edge of denim, leaving the rest for the main piece.

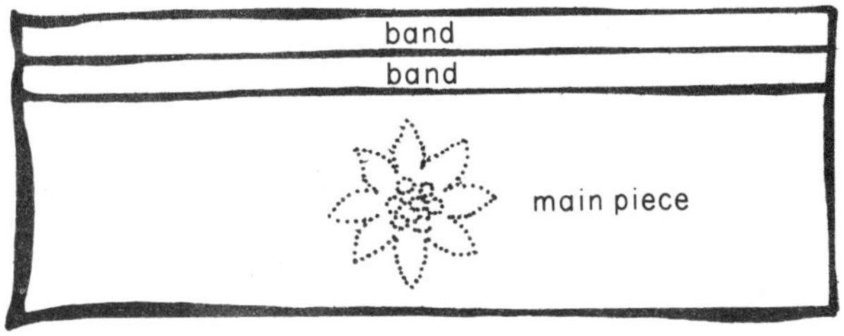

Making up Cut the bottle 10 cm (4 in) from the bottom using household scissors or a knife. Mark centre of main piece and bleach design there. (Or you can repeat the motif several times.) Stick to outside of bottle, folding under short edges to neaten. Make strips into bands, light side as right side. Use to neaten top and bottom edges of pencil holder.

Wastepaper bin

Cover a catering size tin, or a large coffee tin, in the same way. Be sure to hammer down any sharp edges.

Bits-and-bobs box

Materials Empty household match box, or other box approximately 7 × 12 cm ($2\frac{1}{4} \times 4\frac{3}{4}$ in); piece of denim 25 × 18 cm (10 × 8 in); adhesive.
Cutting out Cut two 2.5 cm (1 in) strips from longer edge, leaving rest for main piece.

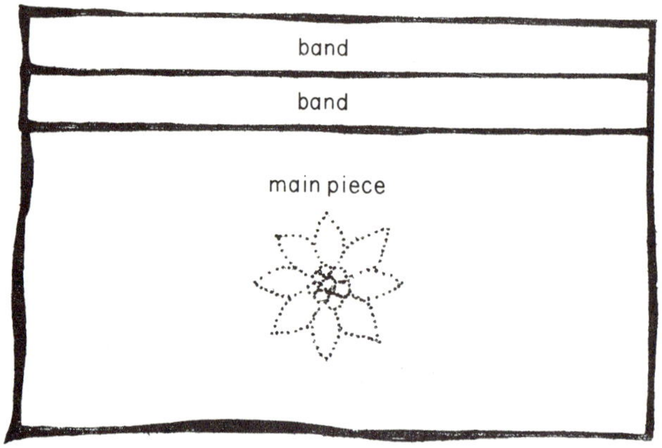

Making up Wrap main piece of denim round box and mark centre of top. Bleach design. Stick round box, folding under shorter edges to neaten. Make strips into bands, light side as right side. Use these to neaten ends of box.

Writing case

This will be 17 × 25 cm (8 × 12 in) when finished.
Materials 0.50 m ($\frac{5}{8}$ yd) denim; two pieces of thick card, each 15 × 25 cm (7 × 12 in); adhesive; writing pad and envelopes.
Cutting out Cut denim between selvedges to give two pieces, each 45 × 50 cm (18 × 22 in). From one piece cut 45 × 15 cm (18 × 8 in) for the first pocket, leaving 45 × 35 cm (18 × 14 in) for the outside cover. From the other piece cut 45 × 20 cm (18 × 10 in) for the second pocket, leaving 45 × 30 cm (18 × 12 in) for the inner cover.

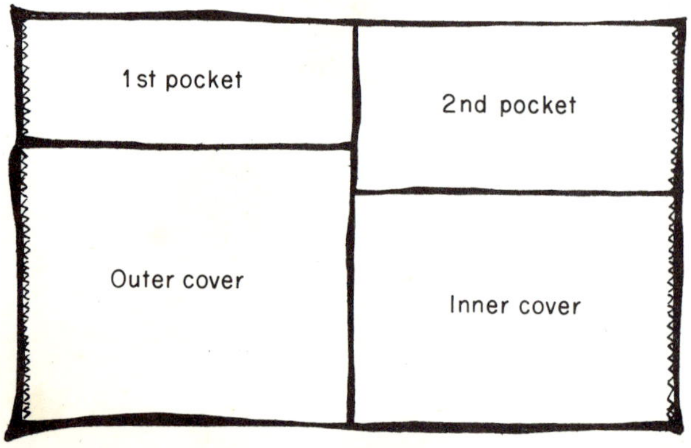

Making up Fold outside cover in half, mark centre of one half, and bleach design. Stick piece of card to wrong side of each half, leaving 5 cm (2 in) between the cards to make the spine, and 2.5 cm (1 in) margins on other edges. Stick inner cover to other side of cards, light side up. Trim this piece to size of cards.

With light side as right side, stick 1 cm ($\frac{3}{8}$ in) hems on one long side of each pocket piece. Put adhesive close to edge of other sides on second pocket. Making sure that the design is on the front cover, press second pocket into place. Stick the spine. Add first pocket in the same way. Turn hems on outside cover to conceal raw edges of pocket and inner cover. Neaten corners and stick into place. Insert writing pad and envelopes.

If attempting a great deal of resist work put your paste into an icing bag with a writing pipe, or use the small plastic bottles with nozzles supplied with hair colourants.

The Nigerians use flour paste as a resist to produce their distinctive fabrics. In Java the form of resist is called batik and involves hot wax. To produce batik at home, melt candles over a gentle heat in a tin can standing in a pan of water. Make sure children cannot upset it when your back is turned. When hot enough to penetrate denim, apply to fabric with a brush. Warm up the wax from time to time if necessary. When the wax has set, brush on the bleach. To remove wax – scrape off as much as possible, then iron between several sheets of newspaper. Finally wash in detergent and press. Using either method of resist you can apply extra paste or wax to the design and bleach again. This produces three shades. Very subtle effects can be obtained by bleaching the light side of the denim.

PAINTING

Painting can be used to decorate most things, but will not stand up to a great deal of hard wear, or careless washing. It is easily added to ready made garments.

Choosing your own designs
Look through magazines and books for suitable designs. Those with blocks of colour and a minimum of detail are effective, and easy to do. Linear designs are difficult to do well and are more suited to embroidery. Good sources of designs are books on folk art and on cultures such as the Aztecs and Incas, also children's books with bold illustrations. The size of the original is not important – but its proportions are – a long narrow design will not fill a square space effectively. The designs given in the section on appliqué can easily be adapted.

Enlarging and reducing designs
Cut a piece of paper to the size of the finished design. Trace original and fold tracing into sixteen rectangles, four each way. Fold paper in the same way. Copy design rectangle by rectangle. (For a larger design you might find it easier to fold the tracing and the paper into sixty-four squares, eight each way.)

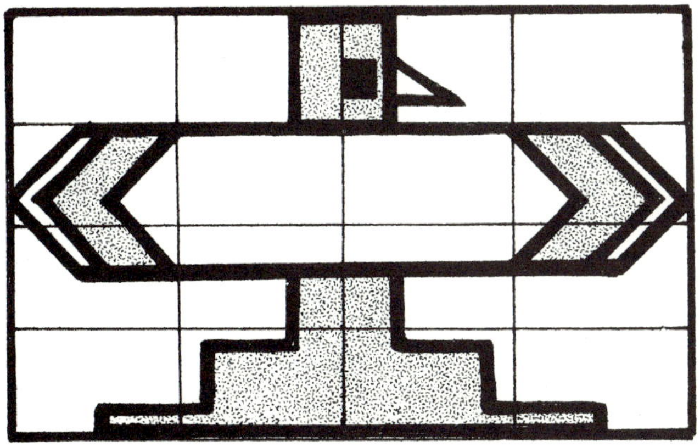

Placing design
Avoid placing designs on the knees or elbows of garments, or anywhere that they will be rubbed, such as seams. Allow a suitable margin around a design. This is particularly important on jackets where only part of the back shows when the garment is on. When estimating the size of a finished design remember to allow for fabric that will eventually be included, or covered, by seams and hems.

Fabric paints
There are several makes of fabric paint readily available. Some are water based (i.e. water is used to remove splashes and to clean brushes) and some are oil based (i.e. white spirit is used for cleaning). If paints are intermixable you will need fewer colours – orange, purple and green can be mixed, as can shades of one colour. Normally the paint is fixed with a hot iron, but check manufacturer's instructions.

Equipment
a piece of board slightly bigger than the design
a piece of polythene sheet the same size
drawing-pins
fabric paint in chosen colours plus white and optional black
saucers
paint brush or brushes
carbon paper
sponge in a saucer of water (white spirit for oil-based paints)

Technique
Wash denim thoroughly to remove dressing. Otherwise the paint will flake. Dry and press. Spread denim over board, light side up, and pin in place. Transfer main outline of design, using carbon and mask. Mark corners of design carefully so that you can replace the design in exactly the same position later on. Place polythene over denim and cut out piece covering design to leave a mask against splashes. Pin in place. Open jar of white paint and stand it in a saucer (in case it is spilled). Squeeze some paint into saucer if it comes in tubes. Paint entire area within outlines with white paint. This makes the

Painted jacket (instructions for making up are in section on Appliqué)

colours brighter and more intense. Allow this base coat to dry. Clean brush.

Replace carbon, mask and design using marks to position them correctly. Pin into place and transfer entire design to denim. Remove carbon etc. and replace polythene mask, then paint in coloured areas. Be sure to cover carbon lines and to clean brush between colours. Use sponge to mop up any splashes as soon as they occur. Add another coat of paint if necessary but do not let the paint layer become too thick or it might crack. Adding a black outline to the main areas of the design makes the colours more brilliant, and gives a stained glass window effect. Allow paint to dry thoroughly, then remove from board. Fix paint as directed.

PRINTING

Printing is an easy and effective technique, suited to most purposes. It will not stand excessive wear or careless washing. It is the easiest way of adding border designs to articles and can be used to imitate some forms of embroidery. The results lack the brilliance of painted denim. I find printing most effective on the lighter side of denim, using dark rather than pale colours.

You can print with many things – for textures try the ends or sides of spent matches, a piece of sponge or an old toothbrush. Use the end of a ruler to duplicate straight embroidery stitches, the rims of tins, pots and bottles to make circles. The ends of cotton reels or nail or screw heads make patterns in their own right. A potato masher can be the basis of a large design – you can print with the potatoes too. Collect as many things as possible and experiment on oddments of denim. Paint can be removed (before it dries) with water or white spirit, but it can stain some plastics and wood, so choose metal objects or things that can be thrown away afterwards.

Equipment

a piece of board slightly larger than the design
a piece of polythene sheet of the same size
newspaper
drawing-pins
fabric paints
saucers
brush
chalk
sponge in saucer of water (white spirit to oil-based paints)

Technique

Wash denim thoroughly to remove dressing, otherwise the paint will flake. Dry and press. Spread several layers of newspaper over the board to give a soft and resilient pad, or use a piece of thin polyurethane foam. Place denim over this, light side up and pin in place. Mark out design with chalk, using a ruler if necessary. Place polythene over denim and cut out piece covering design to leave a mask against splashes. Put the things you are going to print with on newspaper close at hand.

Open the jar of paint and stand it in a saucer – in case it is spilled. (Squeeze some paint into a saucer if it comes in tubes.) You can brush the paint onto the edge of the object, or dip the object straight into the paint. (Small objects can be dipped straight into the jar but for larger objects pour paint into the saucer.) Using a brush gives best results but you must have a brush for each colour or clean the brush each time you change colour. Dipping the object is quicker, but you must still clean the object between colours – and be careful not to dip it in too far or the paint will get all over your fingers. Then, unless you clean your hands immediately, you end up with finger prints everywhere.

Use a sponge to mop up any splashes as soon as they happen, and another sponge, or tissues, to clean objects between colours. When decorating bought clothes, insert a board between the layers of fabric, or you will find traces of paint where you do not want them. For sleeves, pockets, or other awkward places, cut heavy card to shape and slip inside.

I decorated the following collection of boxes in red and white and use them to hold my sewing equipment – but I am sure you will find them useful for many other things: jewellery for instance.

Large tin

Materials 0.7 m ($\frac{3}{4}$ yd) of any weight denim; round or square tin up to 25 cm (10 in) across and 15 cm (6 in) deep; 25 cm (10 in) square of polyurethane foam (optional); adhesive.
Cutting out Wash and press denim. Cut three 2.5 cm (1 in) strips across width of denim. Measure depth of tin from bottom rim to lip. (Not to top rim or the lid will not go on.) Cut a strip this depth. On remaining fabric, mark round lid and cut out leaving 2.5 cm (1 in) all round. If used, mark out foam to exact size of lid. Cut out using household scissors.

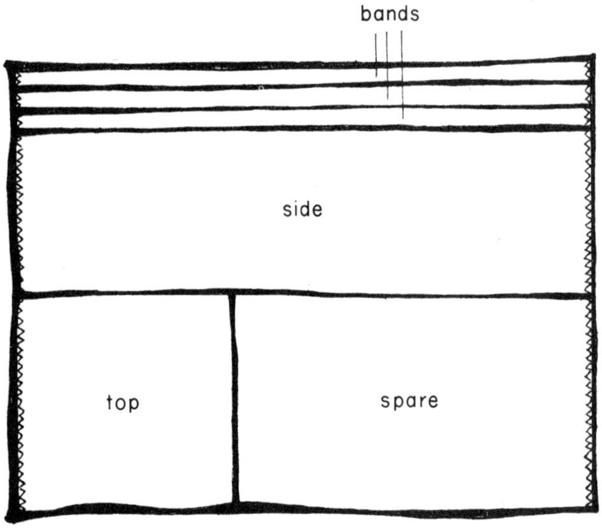

Making up On light side of denim, mark 1.5 cm ($\frac{1}{2}$ in) margins on both long edges of piece for sides, and a 2.5 cm (1 in) margin on piece for lid. Print fabric and fix paint. (I used a potato masher for the centre of the large flower and surrounded it with circles printed with tin lids. A cork made the centre of the small flowers – with the end of a ruler for the petals. The ruler also made the zigzag lines and a match the spots.) Stick denim to sides of tin, fold under shorter ends to neaten. Stick foam, if used, to lid of tin. Stick denim to lid of tin. Stick down edges. Make strips into bands, dark side as right side. Use two to neaten top and bottom edges of tin. (Make sure the lid still fits.) Use third band to neaten edge of lid. Use spare denim to cover a smaller tin or box, or make a pouch.

Small tin

I use this to hold pins, and as a pin cushion.
Materials 45 × 15 cm (18 × 6 in) of any weight denim; small tin or plastic pot, with lid, up to 7.5 cm (3 in) across (the sort used for herbs and spices is ideal); 7.5 cm (3 in) square polyurethane foam (optional); adhesive.
Cutting out Wash and press denim. Cut a 30 cm (12 in) piece across width. From the longer edge of this, cut three 2.5 cm (1 in) strips, and a fourth strip the depth of the tin, minus the lid. On the remaining fabric mark round lid and cut out leaving 2.5 cm (1 in) all round. If used, mark out foam to exact size of lid. Cut out using household scissors.

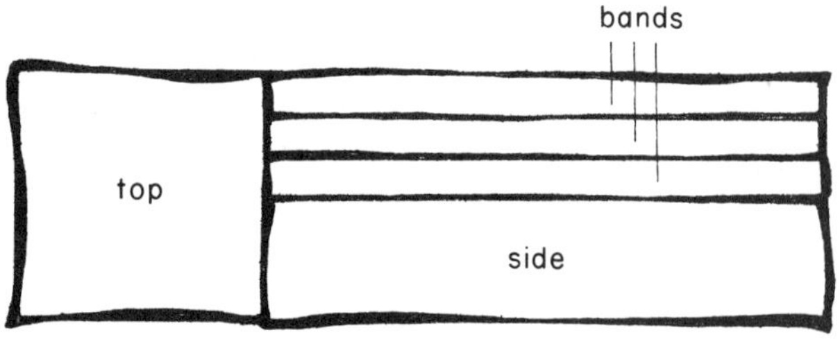

Making up Make up as for large tin, but you might have to trim the denim from the edges of the lid and make the top band slightly narrower. The end of a ruler can be used to make the small flowers.

Box

I use this to hold carbon paper and chalk, but it could as easily hold trinkets and jewellery.
Materials 0.3 m ($\frac{3}{8}$ yd) of any weight denim; cigar box, or tin, up to 25 × 15 cm (10 × 6 in) and 5 cm (2 in) deep; 25 × 15 cm (10 × 6 in) polyurethane foam (optional); adhesive.
Cutting out Wash and press denim. Cut one 2.5 cm (1 in) strip (for top band) and one 5 cm

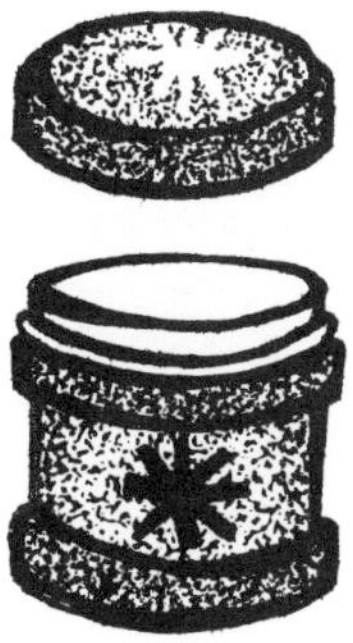

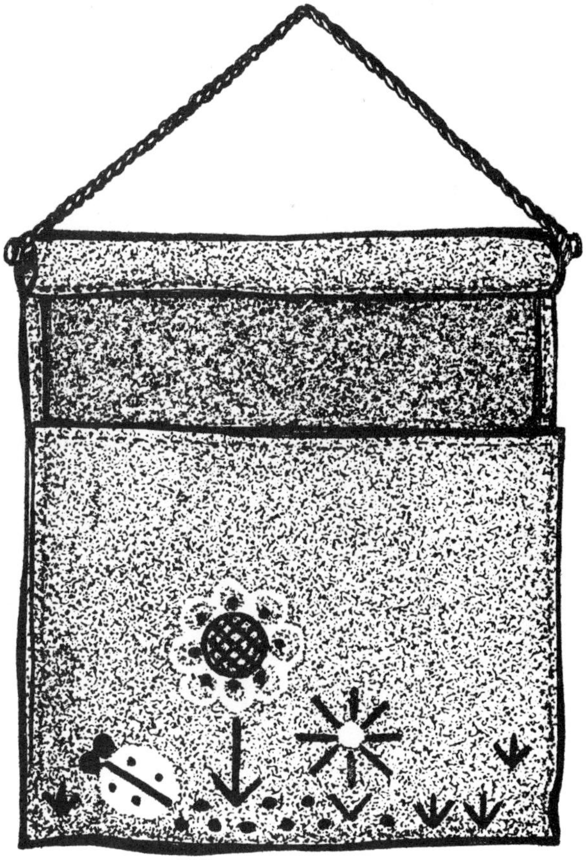

Small tin, box, large tin (top and side), and wall pocket

(2 in) strip (for bottom band), from width of fabric. On remaining fabric mark round lid of box and cut out leaving 2.5 cm (1 in) all round. If used, mark out foam to exact size of lid. Cut out using household scissors.

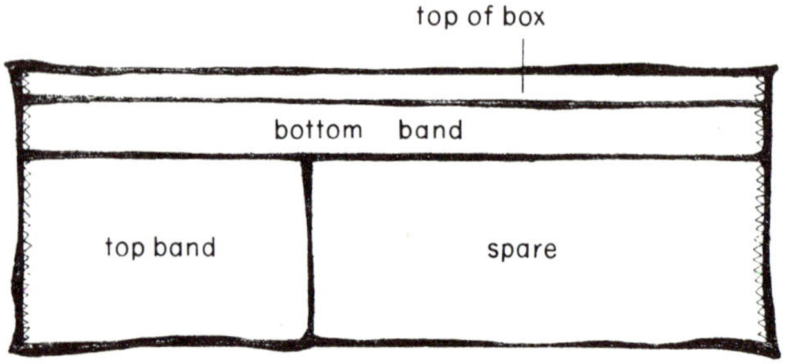

Making up On piece to cover lid, mark 2.5 cm (1 in) margins. Print denim and set paint. Tin lids can be used for the butterfly's wings, and a cork for its spots; the end of a ruler and the end of a match can make the antennae. Stick foam, if used, to the lid. Stick denim to the lid. Stick down the edges. Make strips into bands, dark side as right side. Use narrow band to neaten edge of lid, and wide band to cover sides of box. Spare denim can be used to cover a smaller box or tin, or you could adapt the instructions for the bits-and-bobs box on page 20 and print the top.

Wall pocket

I use this to hold the article on which I am working. I used the bottom of a yoghurt pot for the ladybird's body, a cork for her head, a ruler for her body and a match for her spots. For making instructions see page 29.

TOPSTITCHING

Topstitching is a decorative way of securing hems. Since denim has a dark and a light side, turning hems to the front gives a contrasting border – an effect you cannot get with other fabrics.

Equipment

basic sewing equipment
sewing thread or embroidery thread

Technique

Fold hems to the right side of the fabric. Press and tack. If sewing by hand use running stitch or back stitch, with a matching or contrasting thread or embroidery cotton. Keep stitching straight and close to the edge of the hem. It is more important to keep the stitches even than to keep them small.

If using a sewing machine, first check the tension. Pull top and bottom threads behind the pressed foot. Sew with the hems uppermost. Stitch carefully, using the presser foot or needle plate gauge as a guide, or mark the needle plate with a piece of coloured adhesive tape. You can use a zigzag stitch or machine satin stitch, and if you are lucky enough to have a machine that does automatic embroidery – now is the time to use it.

Denim is hard wearing and an ideal fabric for household table linen. It does not have to be blue, it comes in a range of colours, so you can match your colour scheme. More colour can be added with contrast stitching.

Napkins

These will be approximately 40 cm (16 in) square, but might shrink slightly after washing.
Materials To make four napkins: 0.9 m (1 yd) medium or lightweight denim; thread to match or contrast.
Cutting out Cut fabric into four 45 cm (18 in) squares.

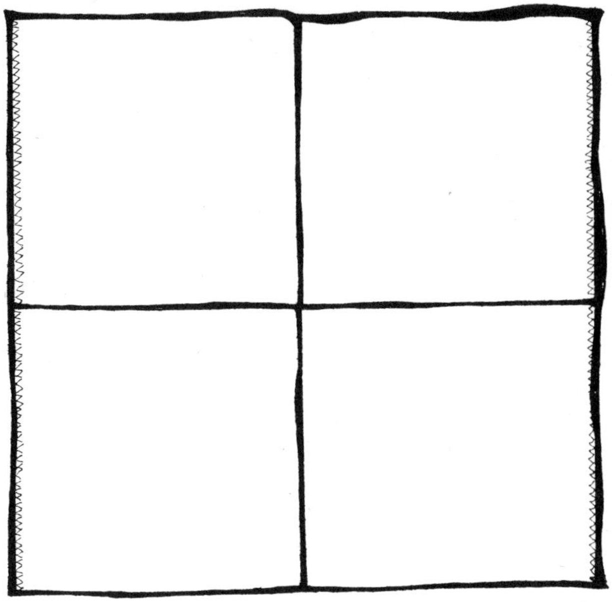

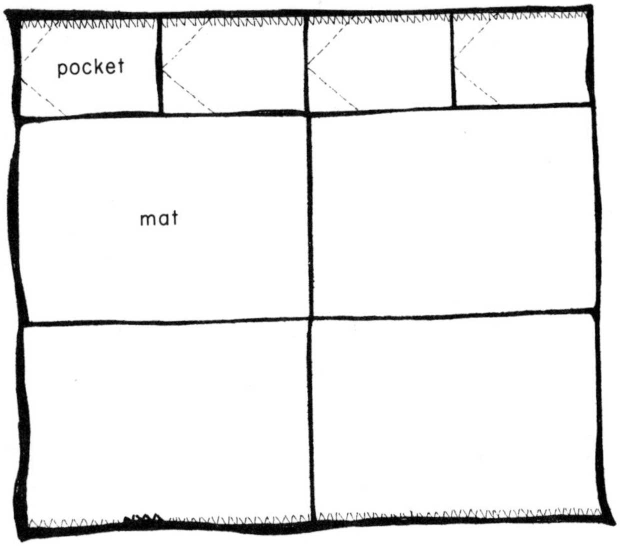

Making up For light napkins with dark edging, use light side as right side. To make dark napkins with light edging, use dark side as right side. Crease 2 cm ($\frac{7}{8}$ in) hems on all edges. Mitre corners. Tack and press. Topstitch; if using a machine sew each napkin in one go. Remove tacking.

Table mats

Made with pockets to hold napkins or cutlery. They will be 45 × 30 cm (18 × 13 in) before washing.
Materials To make four mats: 1 m ($1\frac{1}{8}$ yd) medium or heavyweight denim: thread to match or contrast.
Cutting out Cut a 15 cm (6 in) strip from selvedge. Cut this into four pieces, each 15 × 25 cm (6 × 10 in) for pockets. Cut corners of pockets to give shape shown. Cut remaining fabric to give four pieces, each 37.5 × 50 cm (15 × 20 in).
Making up To make light mats with dark edging, use light side as right side. For dark mats with light edging, use dark side as right side. On pockets, fold 1 cm ($\frac{3}{8}$ in) hems on point and long edges. Mitre corners. Tack and press. Fold 5 cm (2 in) hem on remaining edge. Topstitch this hem only. Make up mats as for napkins. Place pocket at bottom right hand corner of mat, about 1 cm ($\frac{3}{8}$ in) from hems. Tack in place. Topstitch outside and inside edges of pocket. Remove tacking and press.
To make four plain mats, each 40 × 30 cm (16 × 12 in) you will need 0.8 m ($\frac{7}{8}$ yd) of denim.

Large tool kit

To hold full size tools. It will be 35 × 60 cm (14 × 23 in) when unrolled.
Materials 0.7 m ($\frac{3}{4}$ yd) heavyweight denim; 0.7 m ($\frac{3}{4}$ yd) of 2.5 cm (1 in) wide elastic; thread to match or contrast.
Cutting out Cut denim between selvedges to give two pieces, each 45 × 70 cm (18 × 27 in). Keep one piece for outer cover. From second piece cut two 10 cm (4 in) strips, leaving a piece 35 × 60 cm (14 × 23 in) for inner cover.
Making up With light side as right side, join short ends of strips and make into a rouleau to hold the elastic. Thread elastic through casing and secure ends firmly. Place down centre of inner cover, this being dark side up. Arrange tools so the tool kit will roll up properly. Pin between tools. Then remove tools and firmly stitch elastic to cover. Place on top of outside cover, this being light side up. Turn 1.5 cm ($\frac{5}{8}$ in)

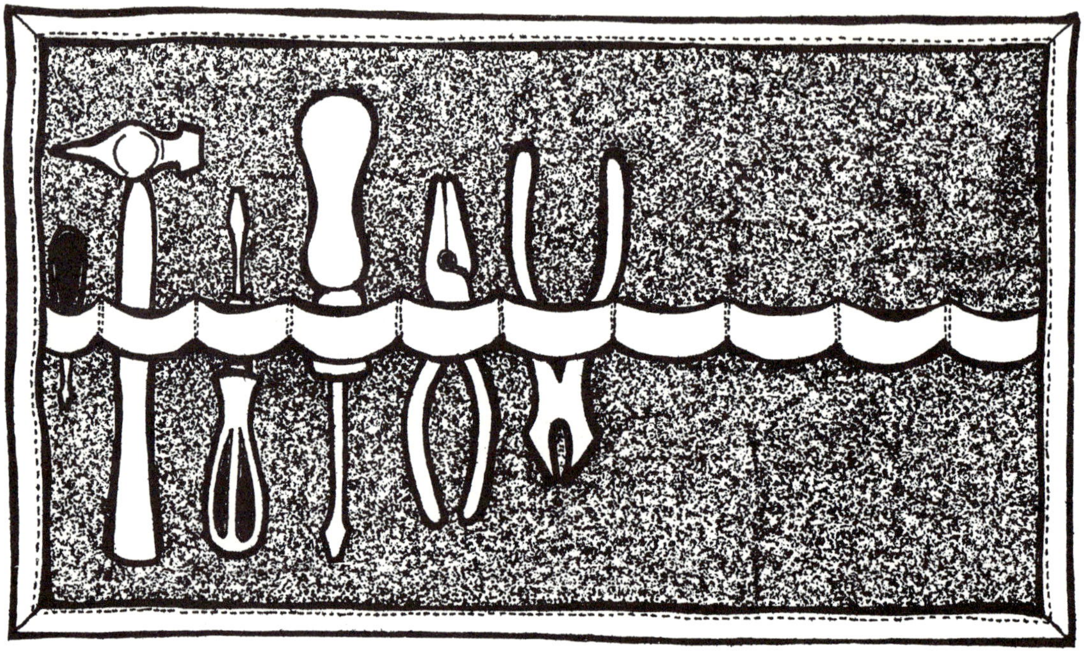

Table mat with pocket, napkin, and large tool kit

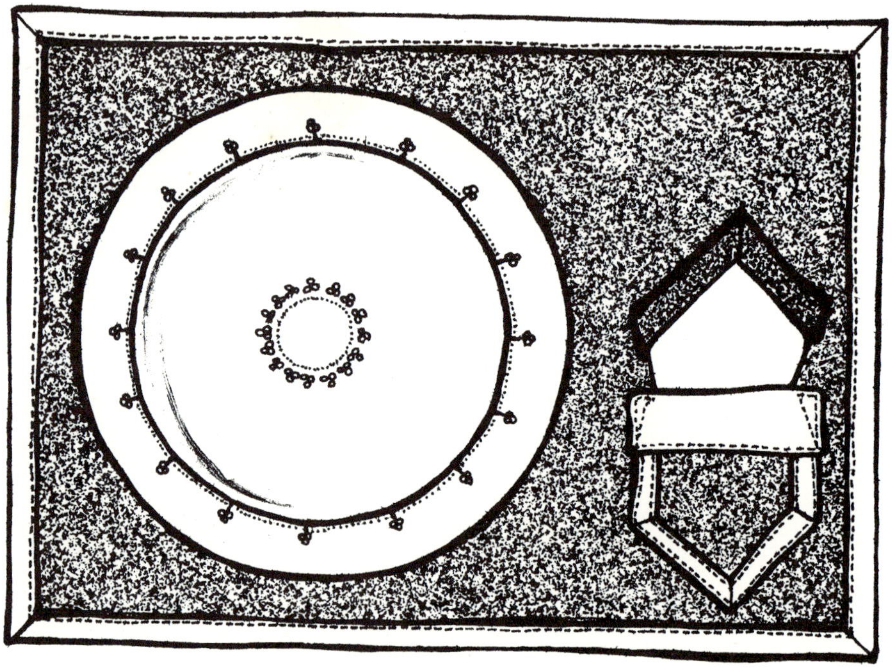

Order your
SIX
free
brochures
now
The choice is yours....
Extra
VALUE BUYS
SPRING/SUMMER '95
SUMMER '95
fashion
UPDATE
SPRING/SUMMER
fashion Experience
HURES NOW ▶▶▶ SEND FOR YOUR FREE BROCHURES NOW

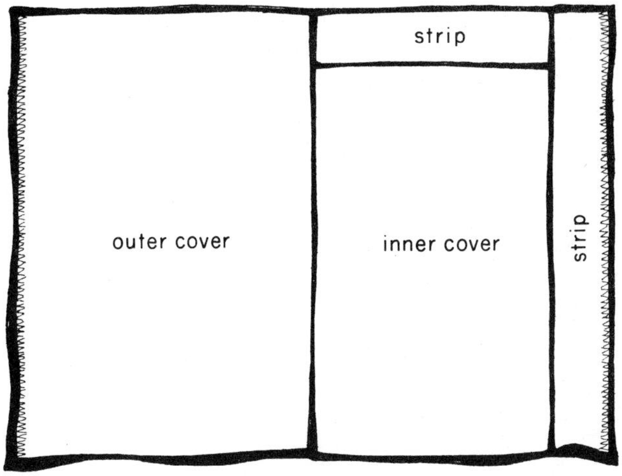

hems over inner cover. Make sure that the hems cover the ends of the elastic. Mitre corners. Topstitch. Remove tacking and press.

Small tool kit

To hold spanners for the car, needlework equipment, or whatever else you can think of. It will be 25 × 40 cm (10 × 16 in) when unrolled.

Materials 0.35 m ($\frac{3}{8}$ yd) medium or lightweight denim; 0.35 m ($\frac{3}{8}$ yd) of 1.5 cm ($\frac{1}{2}$ in) wide elastic; thread to match or contrast.

Cutting out Cut denim between selvedges to give two pieces, each 35 × 45 cm (13$\frac{1}{2}$ × 18 in), keep one piece for outer cover. From second piece cut two 6 cm (2$\frac{1}{2}$ in) strips, leaving a piece 29 × 39 cm (11 × 15$\frac{1}{2}$ in) for inner cover.

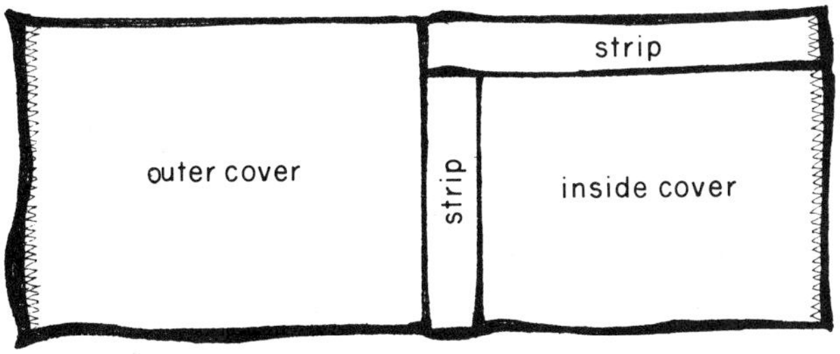

Making up Make up as for large tool kit.

Wall pocket

To hold toys, laundry, knitting, needlework, odds and ends. It will be 40 × 55 cm (16 × 21 in) when finished.

Materials 0.5 m ($\frac{1}{2}$ yd) heavy or mediumweight denim; 0.5 m ($\frac{1}{2}$ yd) wooden dowelling or bamboo cane; 0.75 m ($\frac{3}{4}$ yd) piping or other cord, to match or contrast; thread to match or contrast; sandpaper; adhesive; cold water dye and clear lacquer (optional).

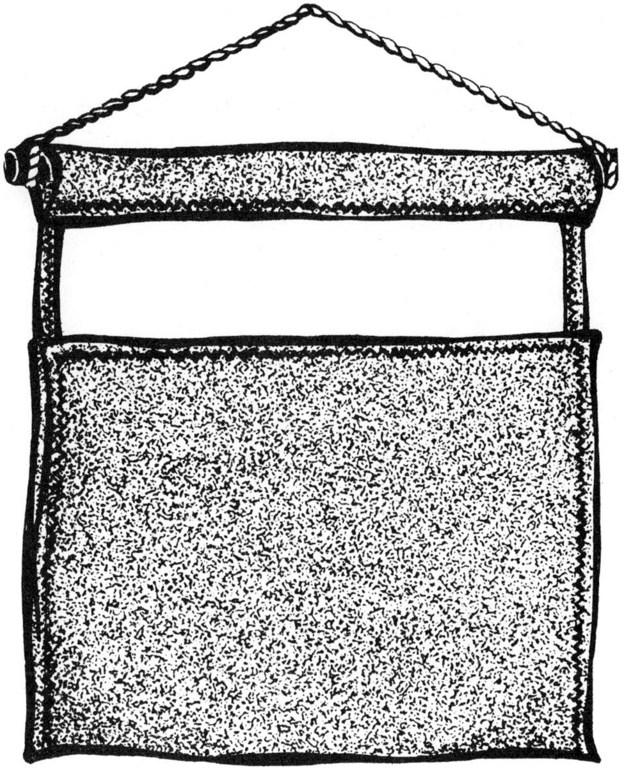

Wall pocket

Making up To make a dark pocket (as illustrated) use light side as right side. For a light pocket, use dark side as right side. With right side uppermost, turn 1.5 cm ($\frac{5}{8}$ in) hems on one short and both long sides. Topstitch. On remaining short side turn a hem big enough for the dowel or cane to go through. Topstitch. Fold 30 cm (12 in) forward from bottom (narrow hem) to make pocket. Tack into place and add another row of topstitching, or oversew into place. Remove tacking and press.

If you want a coloured rod, or need to dye cord, mix dye as directed and leave the rod or cord to soak in it. Follow manufacturer's instructions. (The best way to do this is in an oblong washing-up bowl, or an old baking tin. Prop this up so that the dye collects at one side. You might have to weight the dowel or cane down if it tends to float.) Remove from dye, but do not throw the dye away. Allow to dry and check colour. (Articles always look much darker when wet.) Put back into dye if necessary. When dry, sandpaper lightly, especially the ends, and give two coats of lacquer. Put rod through top hem so that a bit sticks out each side. Tie on cord and stick into place.

You will find it very easy to make this pocket small enough to hold pens and pencils, or large enough to hold the inevitably vast quantities of dirty washing a family piles up.

Tote bag

Tote bag

This should be big enough to carry all your junk, and strong enough to hold the weight of shopping. It will be 45 cm (18 in) high, 30 cm (12 in) wide and 10 cm (4 in) deep. (Remember to remove the card base before washing.)

Materials 0.6 m ($\frac{5}{8}$ yd) heavyweight denim; thread to match or contrast; piece of heavy card 10 × 30 cm (4 × 12 in); adhesive.

Cutting out Cut a 10 cm (4 in) strip across a width of denim. Cut this in half to give two handles, each 10 × 45 cm (4 × 18 in). The remaining denim is for the main part.

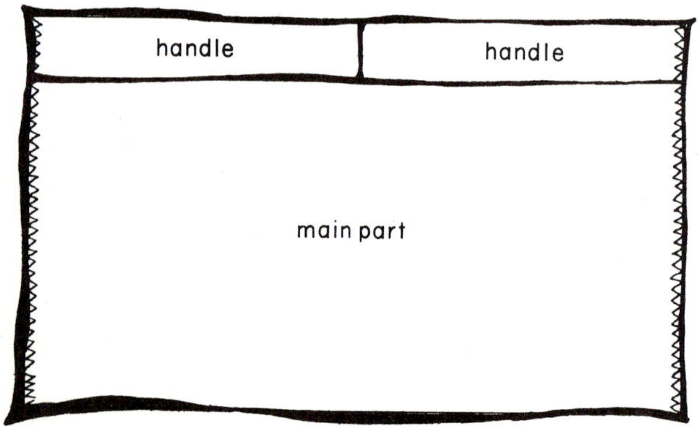

Making up To make a dark bag with light hem, use dark side as right side. For a light bag with dark hem, use light side as right side. Join selvedge edges of main part using a run and fell seam. Turn 5 cm (2 in) hem to right side. Topstitch into place. Turn inside out so that right sides are together and the seam is at one side. Sew 1.5 cm ($\frac{5}{8}$ in) flat seam across bottom edge. Press.

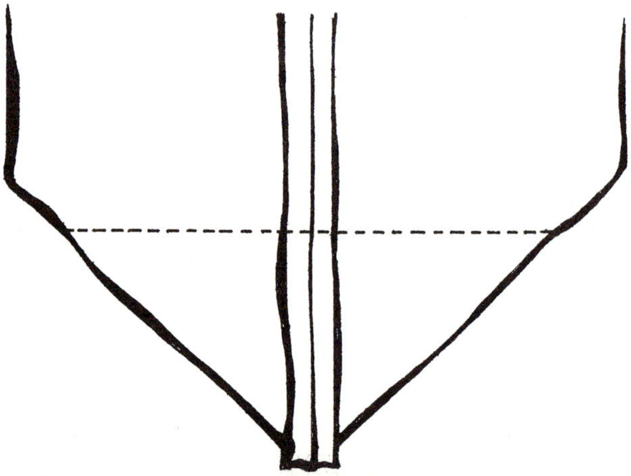

Fold corner of bag so that side seam and bottom seam are on top of each other. Sew across corner. Work other corner to match. Turn bag right side out and push card to bottom of bag to give firm base. (You may have to trim the card to make it fit properly.) Stick card to turned-in corner. Make handles into rouleau. Press, then topstitch both edges. Turn in ends of handles and sew firmly to bag. Add top stitching – for extra looks and extra strength.

You can easily adapt the size of this bag to suit any spare denim you may have, or to fit a particularly shaped object. If you get bored with plain denim, this is a good article to paint, print, appliqué or embroider.

DECORATIVE HEMMING

This is really a prettier form of topstitching, which secures and decorates the hem in one go. It highlights the contrasting borders produced with denim and can be used on any hem, or run and fell seam. It is easily added to ready made clothes – particularly the seams and hems of jeans and jackets.

Equipment
- basic sewing equipment
- crewel needles
- embroidery thread

Technique
The final effect of decorative hemming depends on the thread used. Thick thread gives very bold decoration, and is quickly done. So long as the stitches go through the fold of the hem and the fabric they can be up to 1.5 cm ($\frac{5}{8}$ in) long. It is more important for the stitches to be all the same size than to be small.

Turn hems to the front of denim. Tack and press. Work embroidery. Remove tacking. The best stitches to use are those based on running stitch and back stitch, i.e. threaded, whipped or laced running stitch and pekinese stitch, because you can use two colours. Any form of blanket stitch or buttonhole stitch can be used. Fly stitch and cross stitch are also suitable.

Belt

A plain belt to which one or two pouches can be added. It will be 12.5 cm (3 in) wide.

Materials A piece of heavyweight denim 30 cm (7 in) wide and long enough to go round waist or hips, plus 15 cm (6 in); embroidery thread; 8 eyelets (optional); 60 cm (24 in) shoe lace, or cord, to match or contrast.
Cutting out Wash and press denim. If necessary, trim so that it is 25 cm (6 in) wide and long enough to go round waist or hips, plus 7.5 cm (3 in).
Making up To make a light belt with dark edging, use light side as right side. For a dark belt with light edging, use dark side as right side. Turn 2.5 cm (1 in) hems on all edges. Mitre corners. Tack and press. Work embroidery. Insert or work eyelets, through all three thicknesses of short hems, four each end. Thread through lace or cord, dyed if necessary.

An additional 15 cm (6 in) of denim will make two pouches to attach to the belt. Cut denim in half between selvedges. Then follow instructions for pouch.

Pouch

Adding a cord handle to this pouch makes a child's bag or a neck purse; or the pouch can be added to the belt. It will be 10 × 12.5 cm (4 × 5 in) when finished.
Materials Piece of denim 45 × 15 cm (18 × 6 in); thread to match; embroidery thread, or threads; press stud, or short length of touch fastening: 0.7 m ($\frac{3}{4}$ yd) piping cord or other cord to match or contrast (optional).

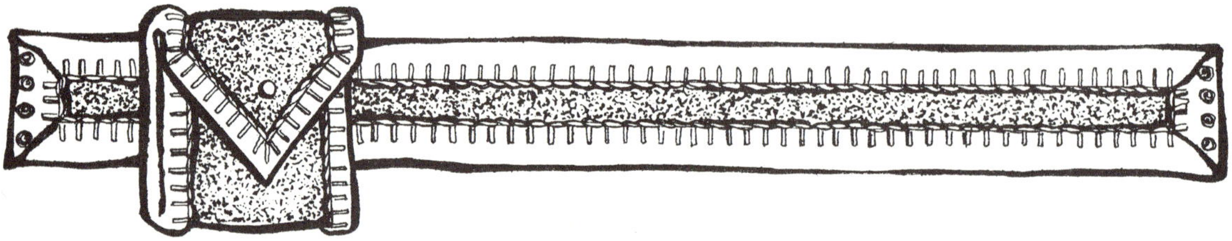

Belt with pouch attached, shoulder bags with different shaped flaps

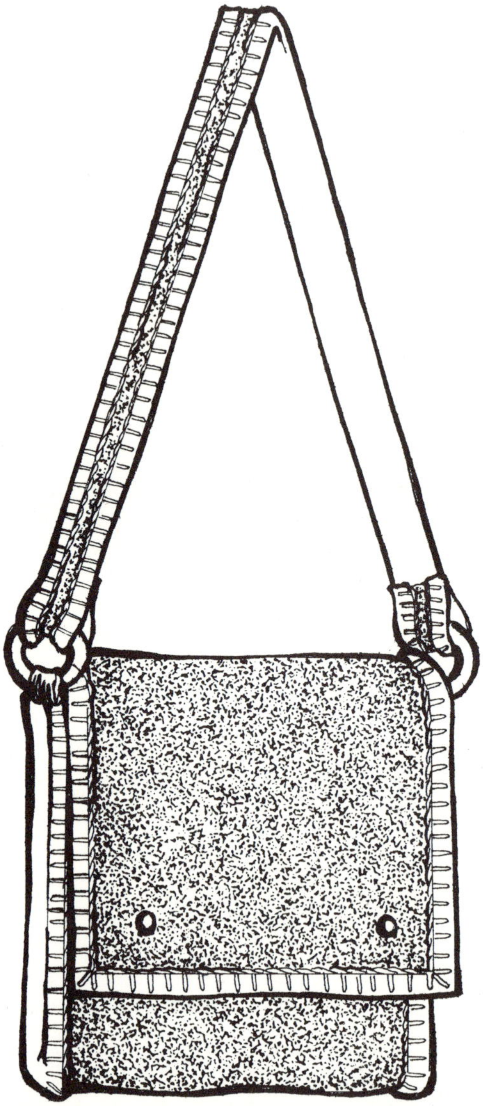

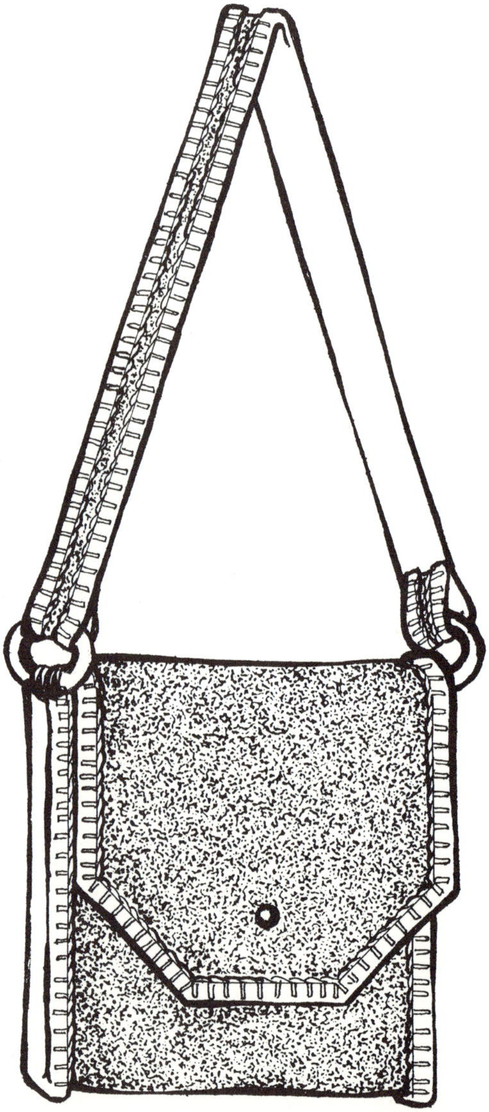

Cutting out Cut corners to shape flap.

Making up To make a light pouch with dark edging, use light side as right side. For dark pouch with light edging, use dark side as right side. Turn 1.5 cm ($\frac{5}{8}$ in) hems on all edges. Mitre corners and tack. Work embroidery. Remove tacking. Fold up 12.5 cm (5 in) to make pocket. Fold over flap and mark position of fastening. Attach fastening. Oversew or topstitch side seam. If used, make knot at each end of cord, and sew knots firmly to corners of pouch. (Cord can be dyed if necessary.) You can easily make this pouch larger or smaller to make good use of a spare piece of denim. Make sure that the denim is roughly three times as long as it is wide.

Shoulder bag

This will be 25 × 30 cm (10 × 12 in) when finished. You can make the flap any shape you like.

Materials 0.50 m ($\frac{1}{2}$ yd) medium or heavyweight denim; thread to match; embroidery thread or threads; press stud, or short length of touch fastening; two large rings.

Cutting out Following diagram 54, cut a 10 cm (4 in) strip across denim to make handle, and a 5 cm ($1\frac{1}{2}$ in) strip to reinforce it. This leaves 34 × 90 cm (13 × 36 in) for the bag. Cut flap to shape.

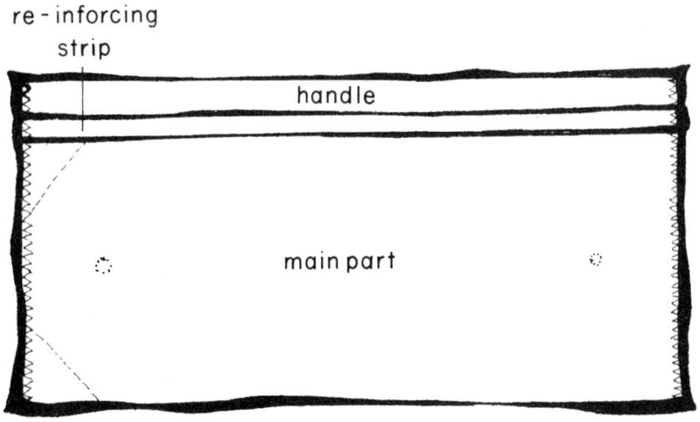

Making up To make a light bag with dark edging, use light side as right side. For a dark bag with light edging, use dark side as right side. Place reinforcing strip down centre of handle. Wrong side of strip to right side of handle. Turn 1.5 cm ($\frac{5}{8}$ in) hems on both long edges. Tack and press. Work embroidery, making sure that the stitches do not show on the other side. Turn 1.5 cm ($\frac{5}{8}$ in) hems on all edges of bag. Mitre corners and tack. Work embroidery. Fold up 30 cm (12 in) to make pocket. Fold over flap and mark position of fastening. Attach fastening. Oversew or topstitch side seam. Sew rings firmly to corners of bag. Thread handle through rings, hemmed side facing out. Make hems at ends of handle to cover rings. Sew firmly.

Small poncho

A small poncho for an adult or a large poncho for a child. It will be 45 cm (18 in) deep.

Materials 0.9 m (1 yd) medium or heavyweight denim; thread to match; embroidery thread or threads.

Cutting out Cut fabric on diagonal to give two triangles.

Making up To make a dark poncho with a light border, use dark side as right side. For a light poncho with a dark border, use light side as right side. With right sides together, make a 2.5 cm (1 in) seam, joining the longest edges of the

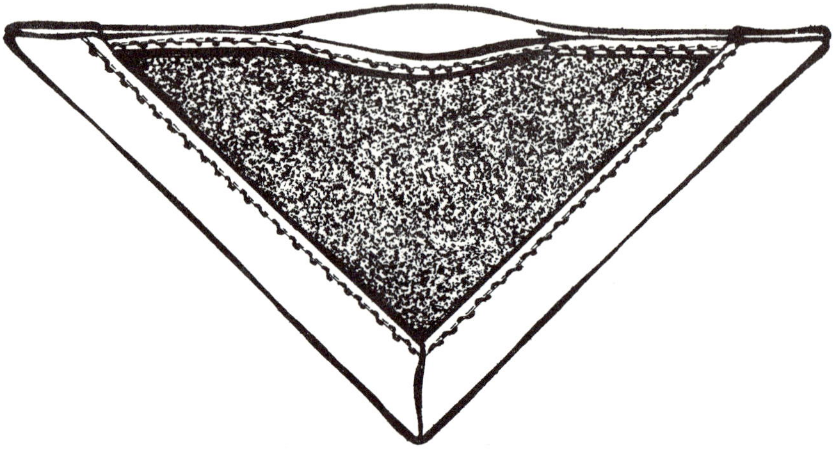

Child's poncho

triangles. Leave 30 cm (12 in) unstitched at centre to make head opening.

Press seam open and make into 1.5 cm ($\frac{5}{8}$ in) hems along entire length. Press and tack. Topstitch or hem into place. Turn 5 cm (2 in) hems on outside edges. Mitre corners. Press and tack. Work embroidery. Remove all tacking.

To make a slightly bigger poncho, make outside hems narrower. For a slightly smaller poncho, turn wider hems. A poncho for a younger child, or toddler can be made in exactly the same way from a smaller square of denim. For a plainer poncho topstitch or hem all edges.

Large poncho

Unless you are very tall, this will cover your knees – and keep them warm. It is 90 cm (36 in) deep.

Materials 1.8 m (2 yd) medium or heavyweight denim; thread to match; embroidery thread or threads.

Cutting out Cut fabric into two 90 cm (36 in) squares. Cut each square along diagonal to give two triangles, making four triangles in all.

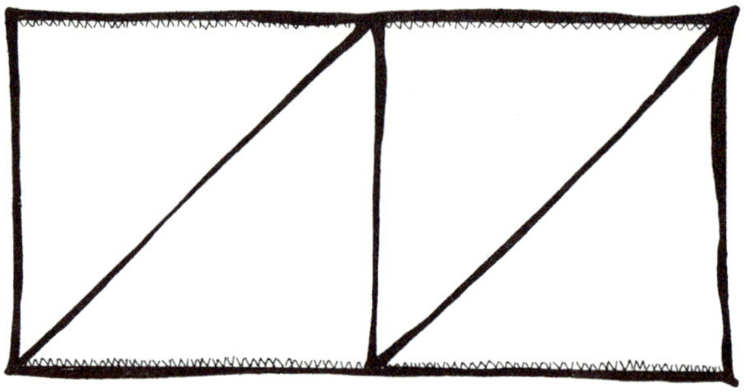

Making up To make a dark poncho with a light border, use dark side as right side. For a light poncho with a dark border, use light side as right side. With right sides together, join two triangles along selvedge, using a 2.5 cm (1 in) seam.

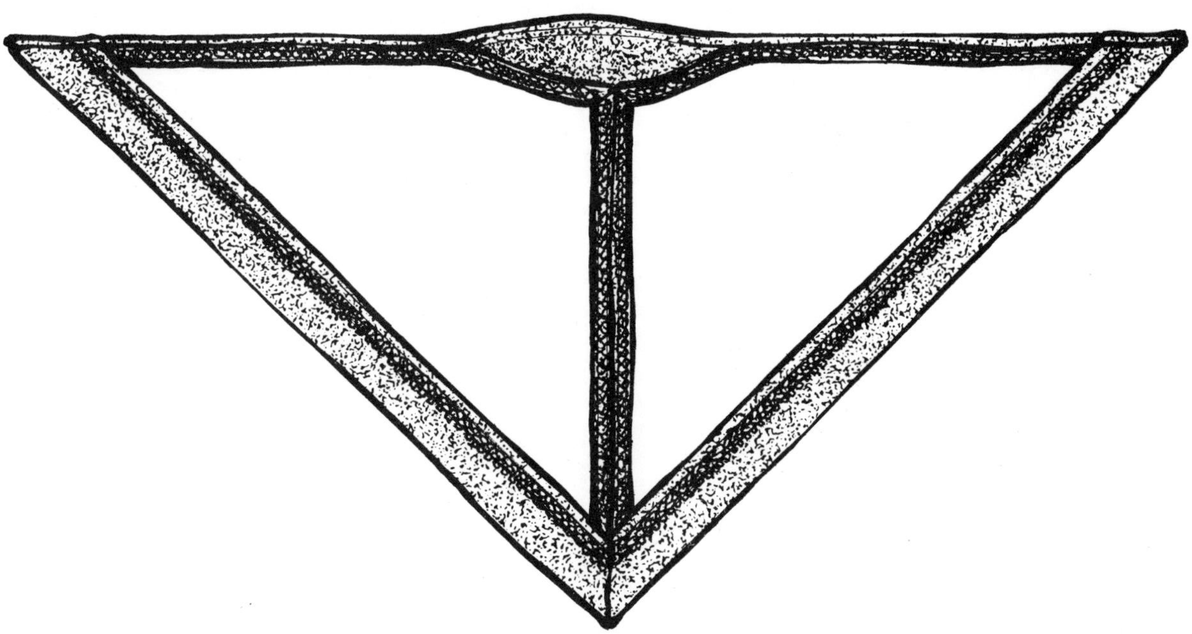

Basic poncho, and basic poncho with appliquéd triangles added and part of one seam left open and folded forward to form revers

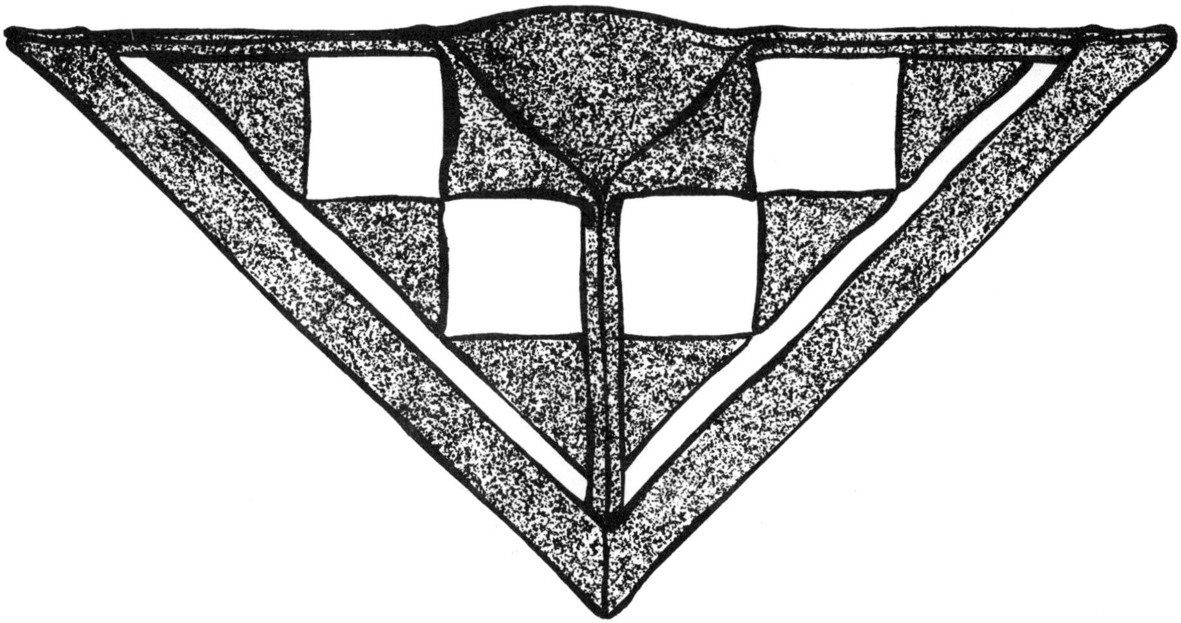

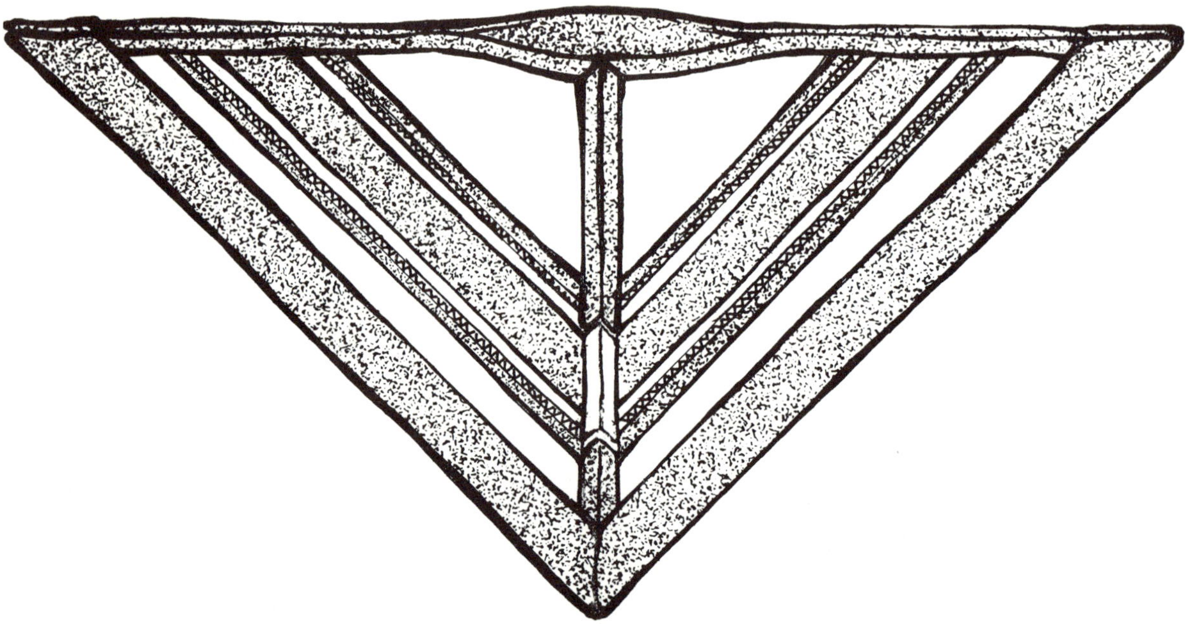

Basic poncho with insets, and basic poncho with plaits made from extra denim added

Repeat with other two triangles. Join longest edges of pairs of triangles. Use a 2.5 cm (1 in) flat seam, right sides together, and leave 35 cm (14 in) unstitched at centre for head opening. Press seams open and make into 1.5 cm ($\frac{5}{8}$ in) hems. Press and tack. Topstitch or oversew into place.
Turn 10 cm (4 in) hems on outside edges. Mitre corners. Press and tack. Work embroidery. Remove all tacking.

You can adjust the length of this poncho by making the bottom hems wider or narrower. Having made your poncho look at the illustrations for ways in which it could be decorated and made more individual.

DECORATIVE SEAMS

This is simply joining two hemmed edges with an insertion or lacing stitch. It depends for its strength and durability on careful stitching, using a strong thread. It should not be used on articles which have to stand up to a great deal of rubbing or tugging. It can be done in two ways.

First method
Materials Basic sewing equipment; sewing thread; strong, twisted embroidery thread or threads.
Technique Turn and stitch hems on edges to be joined. Use matching sewing thread. Using embroidery thread, blanket stitch or buttonhole folded edge of hem. Lace hems together – you can use a contrast thread. You will find diagrams for plain or twisted lacing on page 16. Since the lacing is pulled tight you do not need a paper backing.

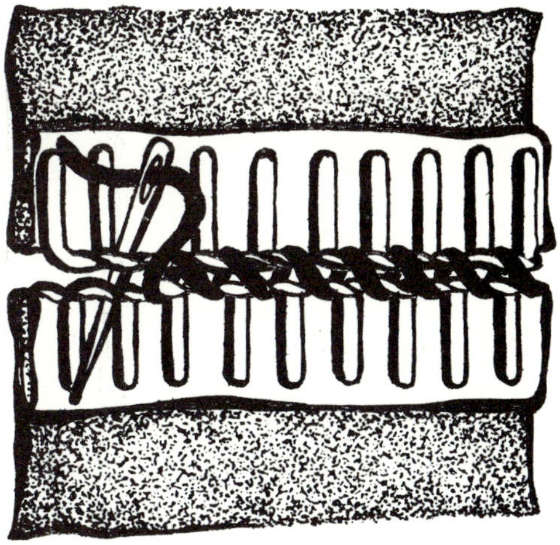

Second method
Materials Basic sewing equipment; sewing thread; strong twisted embroidery thread; cartridge or wrapping paper; household scissors.

Technique Turn and stitch hems on edges to be joined, using matching thread.

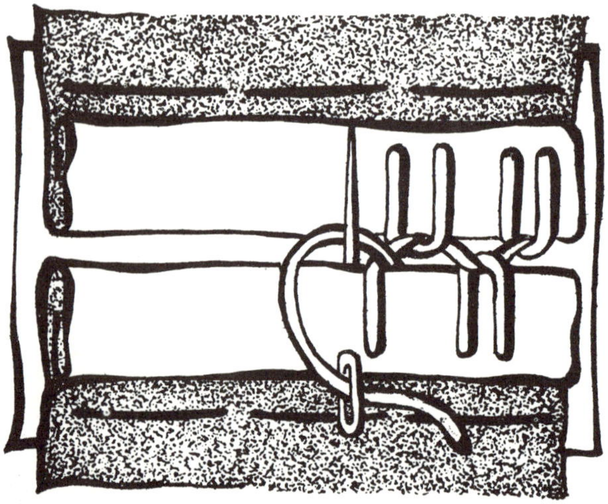

Using embroidery thread join hems using any insertion stitch. You will find diagrams showing how to work faggot and buttonhole insertion on page 16, or you can use cretan stitch as in the diagram above. Make sure that the stitches go through all the layers of the hem and try to keep the thread taut when changing from one hem to the other. The easiest way to keep the stitches even is to mount the hems on paper. To do this, cut a strip of paper at least 5 cm (2 in) wide. Place the denim on this, hems uppermost. Tack denim to paper leaving a small gap between hems. Do not tack too close to the folded edge of the hems or you will find sewing difficult because you have not got enough room to move the needle freely. Find out how wide the gap should be by trying your chosen stitch on spare fabric. It will probably be between 0.25 cm ($\frac{1}{8}$ in) and 0.75 cm ($\frac{3}{8}$ in).

Apron in three sizes

A hardwearing apron in three sizes to provide cover for most shapes and sizes.

Large

For really dirty jobs, or a compliant male. It will be 80 cm (32 in) long.

Materials 1.2 m ($1\frac{3}{8}$ yd) medium or heavy-weight denim; thread to match; embroidery thread or threads.

Cutting out Cut three 10 cm (4 in) strips from width of fabric to make neck band and waist ties. This leaves a 90 cm (36 in) square. From this cut 90 × 25 cm (36 × 10 in) for the lower part of the apron, leaving 90 × 65 cm (36 × 26 in) for the upper part.

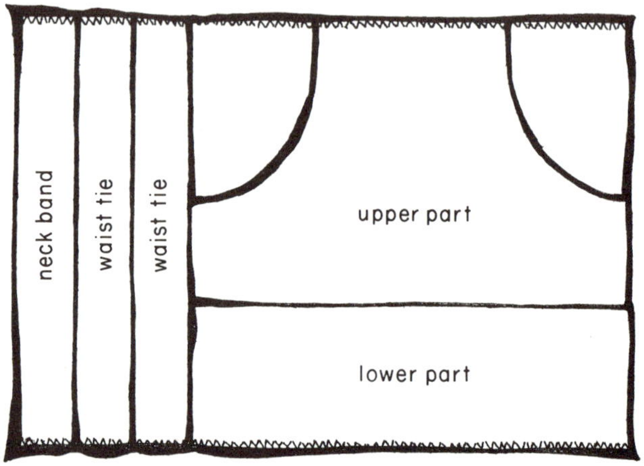

On upper part, mark armholes, 25 cm (10 in) from corner on 90 cm (35 in) edge and 35 cm (14 in) down the 65 cm (26 in) edge. Join these points with a curved line and cut. Cut other armhole to match.

Making up To make a light apron with dark edging, use light side as right side. For a dark apron with light edging, use dark side as right side. Turn and stitch 1.5 cm ($\frac{7}{8}$ in) hems on all edges of lower and upper parts of apron. It is preferable, but not essential to mitre corners.

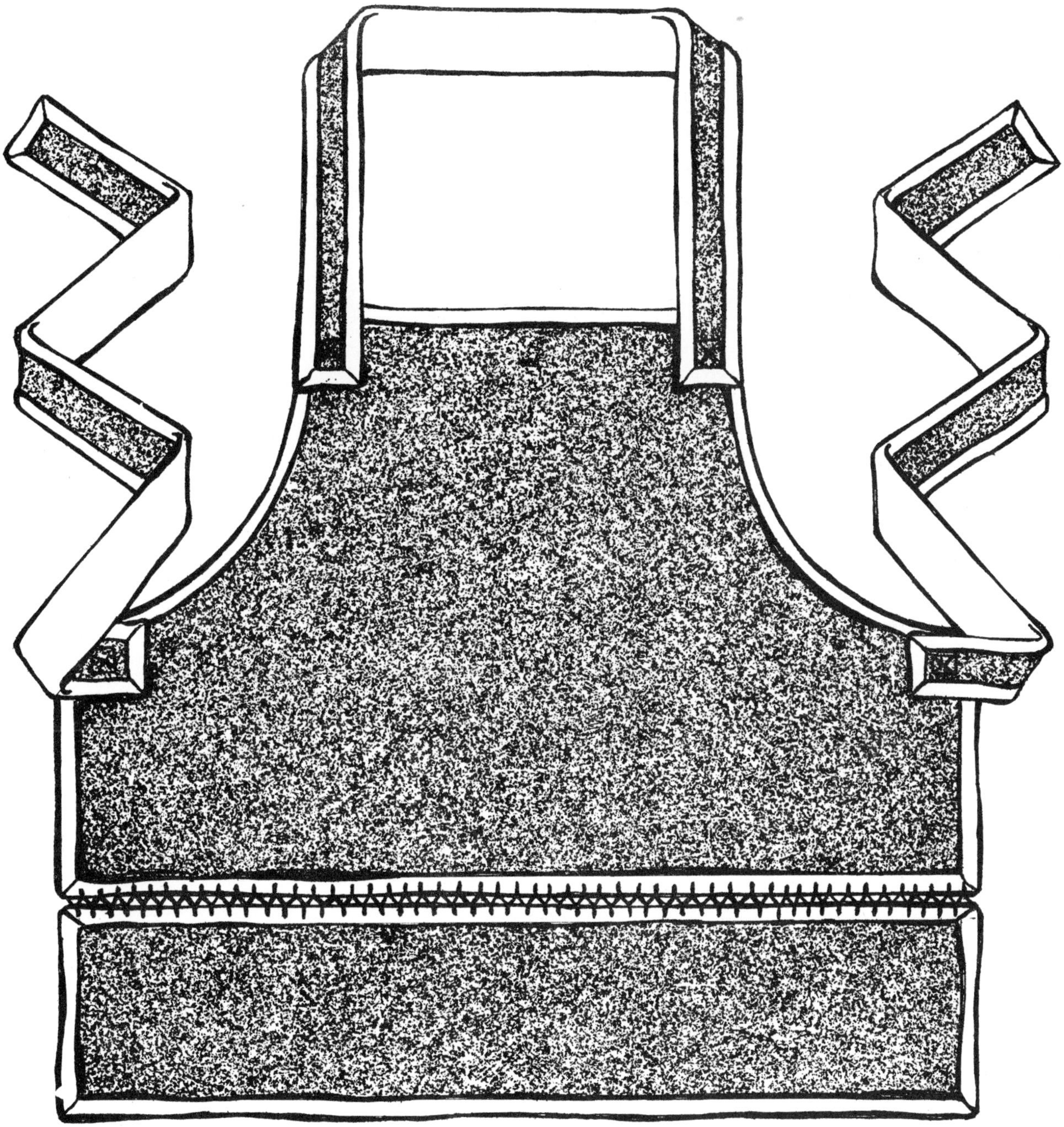

Basic apron

With all hems to the front, embroider seam. Mitring corners will mean you have less thicknesses of fabric to sew at the ends of the seam – it could be hard work on heavy denim.
Turn and stitch 1.5 cm ($\frac{5}{8}$ in) hems on all edges of neck band and waist ties. Attach these to apron, topstitching as shown below. There is no point in a sturdy apron if the ties give way (and it will always be at the wrong moment).

Medium
For everyday chores. It will be 60 cm (24 in) long.
Materials 0.8 m ($\frac{7}{8}$ yd) medium or heavyweight denim; thread to match; embroidery thread or threads.
Cutting out Cut two 10 cm (4 in) strips from selvedge edge for waist ties, and one 10 cm (4 in) strip from width of fabric for neck band. This leaves a 70 cm (28 in) square. From this cut 70 × 20 cm (28 × 8 in) for the lower part of apron, leaving 70 × 50 cm (28 × 20 in) for upper part.

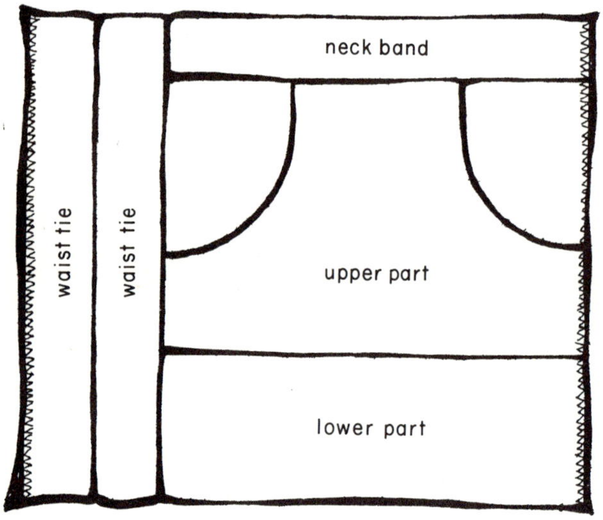

On upper part, mark armholes, 20 cm (8 in) from corner on 70 cm (28 in) edge and 25 cm (10 in) down the 50 cm (20 in) edge. Join these points with a curved line and cut. Cut other armhole to match.
Making up Make up as for large apron.

Small
Suitable for a child or to use as a hostess apron. It will be 50 cm (20 in) long.
Materials 0.6 m ($\frac{5}{8}$ yd) medium or heavyweight denim; thread to match; embroidery thread or threads.
Cutting out Cut three 10 cm (4 in) strips from selvedge to make neck band and waist ties. This leaves a 60 cm (24 in) square. From this cut 60 × 15 cm (24 × 6 in) for lower part of apron, leaving 60 × 45 cm (24 × 18 in) for upper part. On upper part, mark armhole, 15 cm (18 in) down the 45 cm (18 in) edge. Join these points with a curved line and cut. Cut other armhole to match.

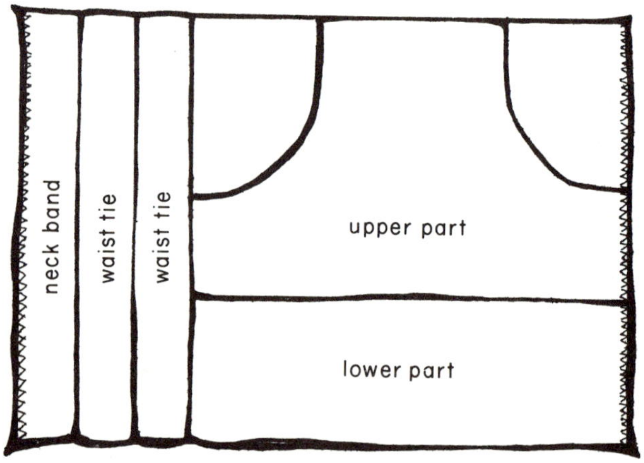

Making up Make up as for large apron.

Plain apron

This is a slightly longer apron with pockets, and does not involve insertion. Buy materials as given for chosen size. Cut ties and neck band, but leave square intact. Cut armholes following instructions. Make up as for large apron. From spare fabric cut patch pockets. Turn and stitch hems on all edges then topstitch into place – or you could use this fabric for an appliqué design.

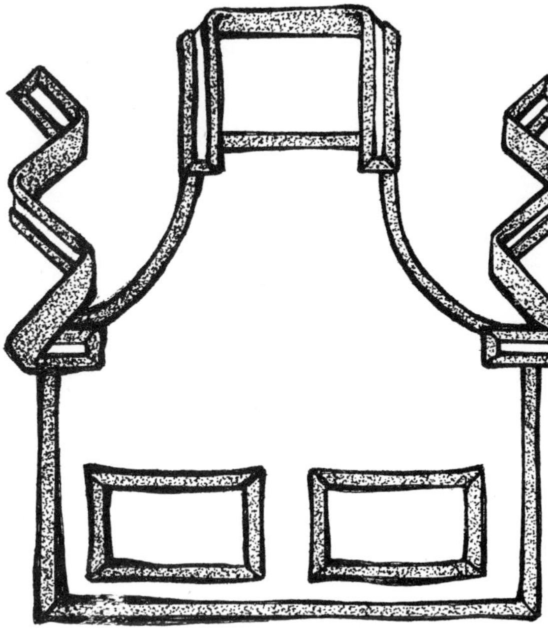

Plain apron

Oversmock in three sizes

These smocks are based on traditional fishermen's smocks. They are hip length with elbow length sleeves. The side slits allow for extra movement. They are in three sizes.

Large

To fit 95–105 cm (38–42 in) bust or chest, length 70 cm (28 in), and sleeve seam 30 cm (12 in).

Materials 2.3 m ($2\frac{1}{2}$ yd) medium or heavy-weight denim. After shrinking this should be at least 2.1 m ($2\frac{1}{4}$ yd); thread to match; embroidery thread or threads.

Cutting out Wash and press denim. It is important to shrink denim before making up. It would be a waste of time making up a smock and not being able to wear it after the first wash. Cut across width into three pieces, each 70 × 90 cm (27 × 36 in). Keep two for back and front. Cut third piece to give two sleeves, each 70 × 45 cm (27 × 18 in).

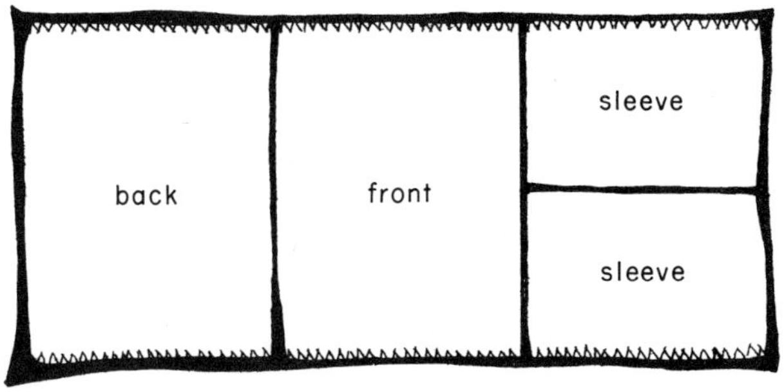

Making up To make a light smock with dark borders, use light side as right side. For a dark smock with light borders, use dark side as right side. On back and front turn and stitch 1.5 cm ($\frac{5}{8}$ in) hems on both long sides, and one short

side. It will be easier to work the embroidered seams if the corners are mitred – you will not have so many thicknesses to sew through.

Turn and stitch 15 cm (6 in) bottom hem. Join shorter edges of sleeves, using a run and fell

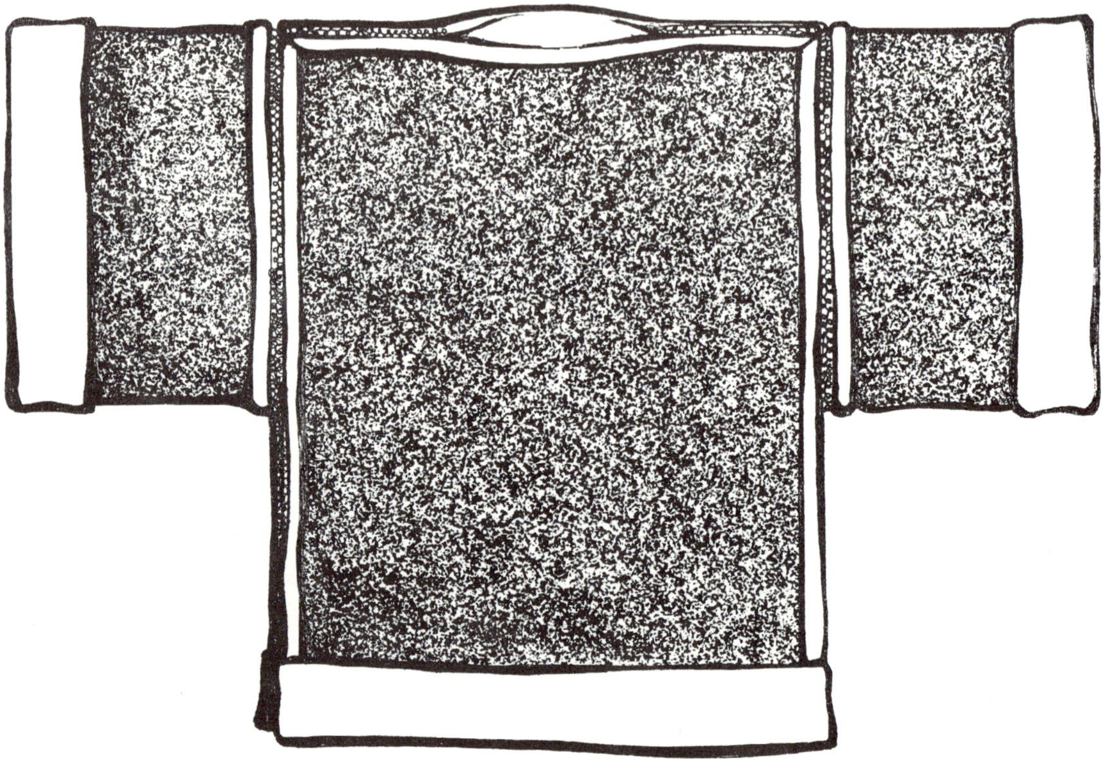

Basic smock, derived from traditional fishermen's smocks. It could be further decorated; the hems could be embroidered, or an embroidered motif could be added; it could also be painted or printed

seam (any other seam will show when you turn the hems). Turn and stitch 1.5 cm ($\frac{5}{8}$ in) hem for shoulder edge and 10 cm (4 in) bottom hem. Embroider top (narrow) hems of back and front to form shoulders. Leave 35 cm (14 in) unstitched at centre for head opening. Join centre of shoulder hem to shoulder seam and embroider seam. Embroider from under arm to join sides. Leave 15 cm (6 in) open. If you want to make a longer smock, turn narrower hems on the bottom of the front and back and sleeves. To make a shorter smock, either make the hems wider or cut a strip from short edge of front and back and longer edge of sleeves.

Medium
To fit 80–90 cm (32–36 in) chest or bust, length 70 cm (28 in), sleeve seam 30 cm (12 in).

Materials 2 m ($2\frac{1}{4}$ yd) medium or lightweight denim. After shrinking this should be at least 1.8 m (2 yd); thread to match; embroidery thread or threads.
Cutting out Wash and press denim. This is important. Then, as for the large oversmock cut across width into three pieces, each 60 × 90 cm (24 × 36 in). Keep two for front and back. Cut third piece to give two sleeves, each 60 × 45 cm (24 × 18 in).

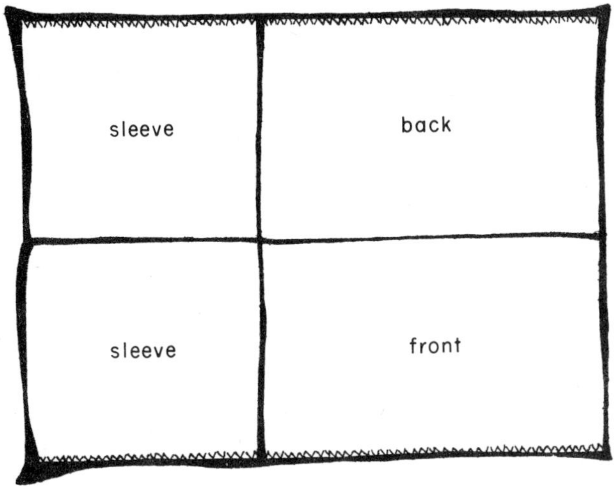

Making up Make up as for large smock, but leave 32.5 cm (13 in) for head opening. Lengthen or shorten as for large smock.

Small
To fit a child, 65–75 cm (26–30 in) chest, length 50 cm (20 in), sleeve seam 25 cm (10 in).
Materials 1.3 m ($1\frac{3}{8}$ yd) medium or heavy-weight denim. After shrinking this should be at least 1.15 m ($1\frac{1}{4}$ yd); matching thread; embroidery thread or threads.
Cutting out Wash and press denim. Cut fabric between selvedges to give two pieces, each 115 × 45 cm (45 × 18 in). From each piece cut 50 × 45 cm (20 × 18 in) for sleeves, leaving 65 × 45 cm (25 × 18 in) for back and front.
Making up Make up as for large smock, but leave 30 cm (12 in) for head opening. This smock can be lengthened or shortened as for large smock, or it can be lengthened by buying extra fabric. Work out how much longer you want the smock to be; buy this amount of extra fabric. Remember to add extra length to back and front, when you cut them out. To shorten, buy less fabric.

DECORATIVE INSETS

This is simple to do, but looks complicated. All you are doing is cutting out a strip of denim, turning it over and sewing it back into place – giving bands of colour. It is an extension of decorative seaming, and is a very useful way of lengthening or letting out garments, especially those that children have out-grown.

First method
Materials Basic sewing equipment; sewing thread; strong twisted embroidery thread, or threads.
Technique Turn and stitch hems on edges to be joined. Make sure that the inset shows the wrong side of the denim. Blanket stitch or buttonhole folded edge of hems. Diagrams showing how to work plain or twisted lacing are on page 16. If the lacing is pulled tight you will not need a paper backing.

Second method
Materials Basic sewing equipment; sewing thread; strong twisted embroidery thread, or threads; household scissors; cartridge or wrapping paper.
Technique Turn and stitch hems on edges to be joined. Make sure that the inset shows the wrong side of the denim.
Join hems using any insertion stitch. Diagrams showing how to work faggot and buttonhole insertion are on page 16, and cretan stitch on page 38. Make sure that the stitches go through all the layers of the hem and try to keep the thread taut when changing from one hem to the other. The easiest way to keep the stitches even is to mount the inset and its joining hems onto paper. To do this cut a strip of paper wide enough to go under the inset and the hems to be joined. Place denim on this with hems uppermost and

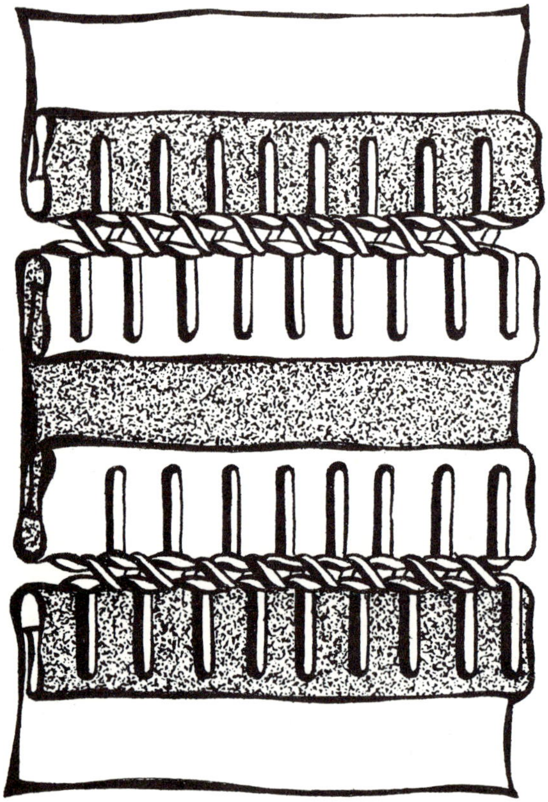

First method

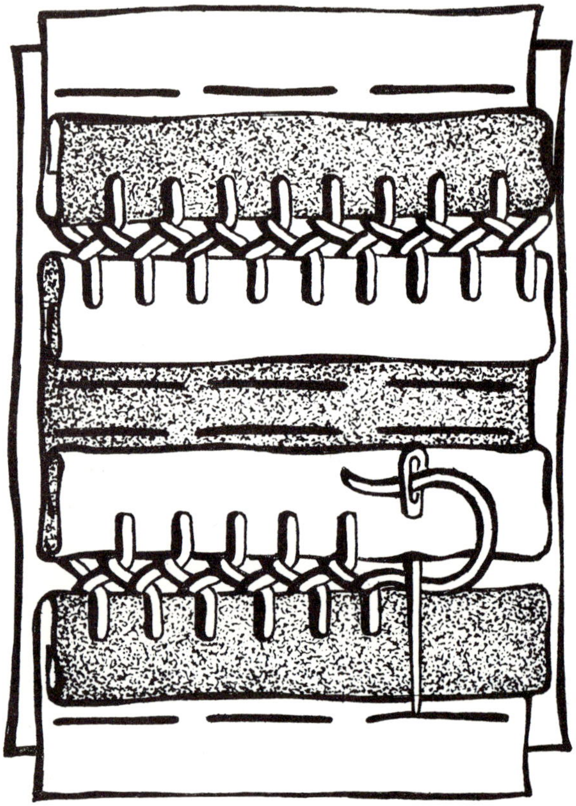

Second method

tack into place, leaving a small gap between the hems. If you tack too close to the hem you will find sewing difficult because you have not enough room to move the needle easily. Find out how wide this gap should be by trying out your chosen stitch on spare fabric. It will probably be between 0.25 cm ($\frac{1}{8}$ in) and 0.75 cm ($\frac{3}{8}$ in).

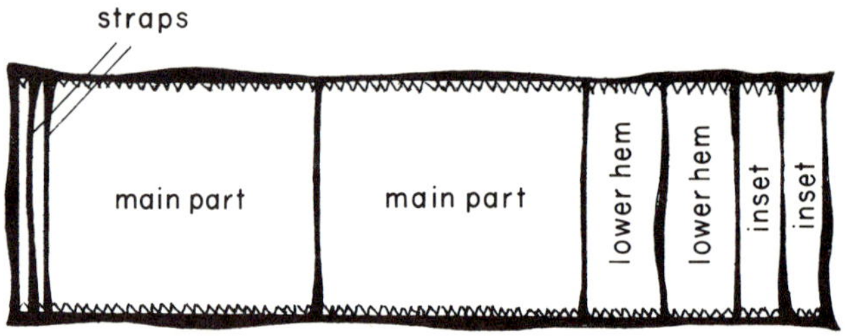

Sun dress or skirt

This can lead a double life as a peasant skirt. To fit 80–90 cm (32–38 in) bust, 115 cm (45 in) long. For this particular garment you will need a sewing machine.

Materials 3.3 m ($3\frac{3}{4}$ yd) medium or lightweight denim – after shrinking this should be at least 3 m ($3\frac{3}{8}$ yd); thread to match; embroidery thread or threads; shirring elastic.

Cutting out Wash and press denim. Then across width cut two 5 cm (2 in) strips for straps, two pieces, each 100 × 90 cm (40 × 36 in) for main part, two pieces, each 30 × 90 cm (12 × 36 in) for lower hems, and two pieces 15 × 90 cm (6 × 36 in) for inset.

Making up To make a dark dress or skirt with light hem and inset, use dark side as right side. For a light dress or skirt with dark hem and inset, use light side as right side. Join longer edges of main part with run and fell seams. Press. Turn and stitch 1.5 cm ($\frac{5}{8}$ in) hems on top and bottom edges. Join short edges of lower hems with run and fell seams. Press. Turn and stitch 1.5 cm ($\frac{5}{8}$ in) hem on top edge and a 10 cm (4 in) hem on bottom hem. Make sure that both hems

Sun dress

are turned to the front. Join short edges of inset with run and fell seams. Turn and stitch 1.5 cm ($\frac{5}{8}$ in) hems, to the wrong side, on both edges. With all hems uppermost, embroider inset to hem of main part. With hems uppermost, embroider narrow hem of lower hem to inset to remaining hem of inset.

Put bobbin into machine and thread top of machine with thread. Wind shirring elastic onto machine bobbin by hand. Mark 2.5 cm (1 in) from remaining hem of main part. With right side of denim uppermost stitch along this line; go round twice for extra strength. (This hem edge makes the frill.) Work six more rows of shirring, 2.5 cm (1 in) apart. Stitch last row twice. (If you have a quilting foot you can use it to keep the rows of shirring parallel, or a card guide, as suggested for hems, works just as well.) Pull up shirring elastic until garment fits fairly tightly round bust and loosely round waist. Fasten off ends of thread and elastic firmly.

Make straps into rouleau and sew firmly to centre of top. Make sure stitching goes through the shirring as well as the frill. The frill itself is not strong enough and may tear – at the wrong moment. To wear as a skirt, tie straps round waist as a belt, or tie them in a large bow. (You could simply tuck them inside.)

To adjust length If you only need to shorten or lengthen this garment slightly, make the lower hem wider or narrower. To lengthen considerably, work out how much longer you want the dress to be, then double this amount. Buy this much extra fabric. To shorten, work out the adjustment, double it, and take this away from the amount of fabric needed. In either case make sure that you add or take away this amount from the longer side of the upper part of garment. (If you do not trust your own maths, cut straps, insets and lower hems first. Then cut remaining fabric in half, across width, to give main parts.)

Child's sun dress or skirt

To fit chest 65–75 cm (26–30 in), length 75 cm (29 in).

Materials 1.6 m ($1\frac{3}{4}$ yd) medium or lightweight denim – after shrinking this should be at least 1.4 m ($1\frac{1}{2}$ yd); thread to match; embroidery thread or threads; shirring elastic.

Cutting out Across the width of denim, cut a 5 cm (2 in) strip. Cut this in half to give two straps, each 45 cm (18 in) long. From the remaining denim, cut a 15 cm (6 in) strip for lower hem, a 10 cm (4 in) strip for inset, leaving a 65 cm (26 in) strip for main part.

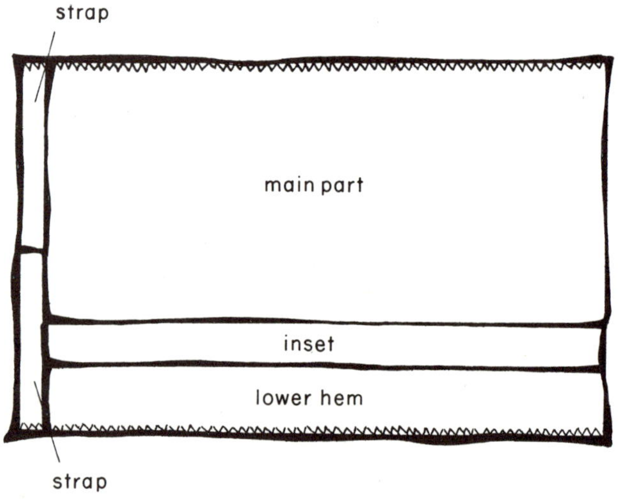

Making up Make up as for adult version, but make bottom hem 5 cm (2 in) wide instead of 10 cm (4 in), and work five rows of shirring instead of seven.

To adjust length To adjust length slightly make lower hem wider or narrower. To shorten considerably, cut a strip from long edge of main part.

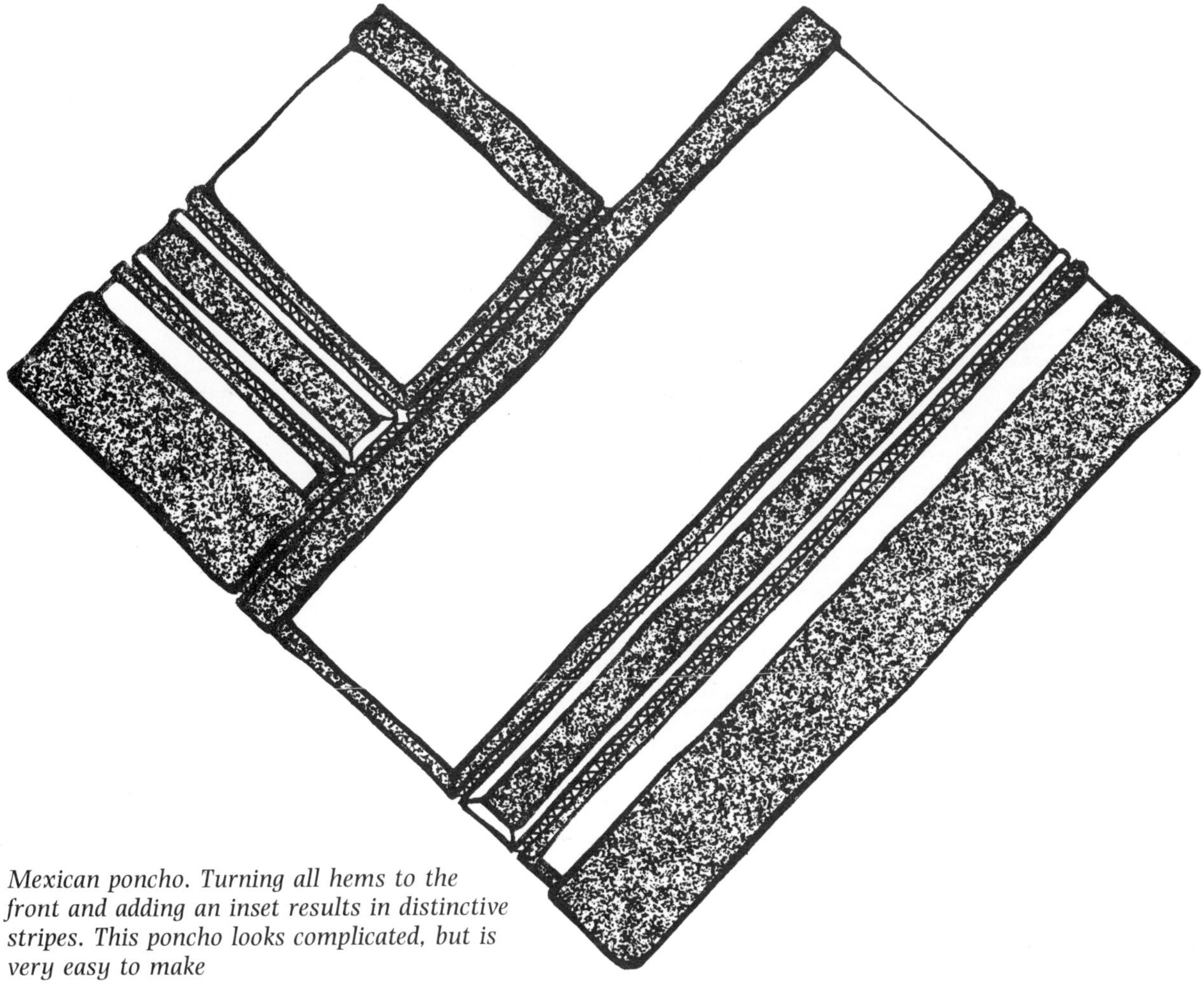

Mexican poncho. Turning all hems to the front and adding an inset results in distinctive stripes. This poncho looks complicated, but is very easy to make

Mexican poncho

This is based on the ponchos worn by Mexican gauchos (cowboys). It measures 45 cm (18 in) over the shoulder and is 60 cm (24 in) deep at centre front and back.

Materials 1.4 m ($1\frac{1}{2}$ yd) heavy or medium-weight denim; thread to match; embroidery thread or threads.

Cutting out Across width of denim, cut two 35 cm (13 in) pieces for main part, two 10 cm (4 in) strips for insets, and two 25 cm (10 in) strips for lower hems.

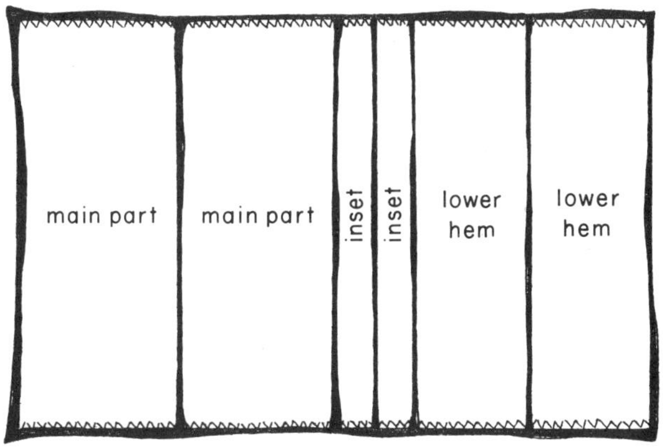

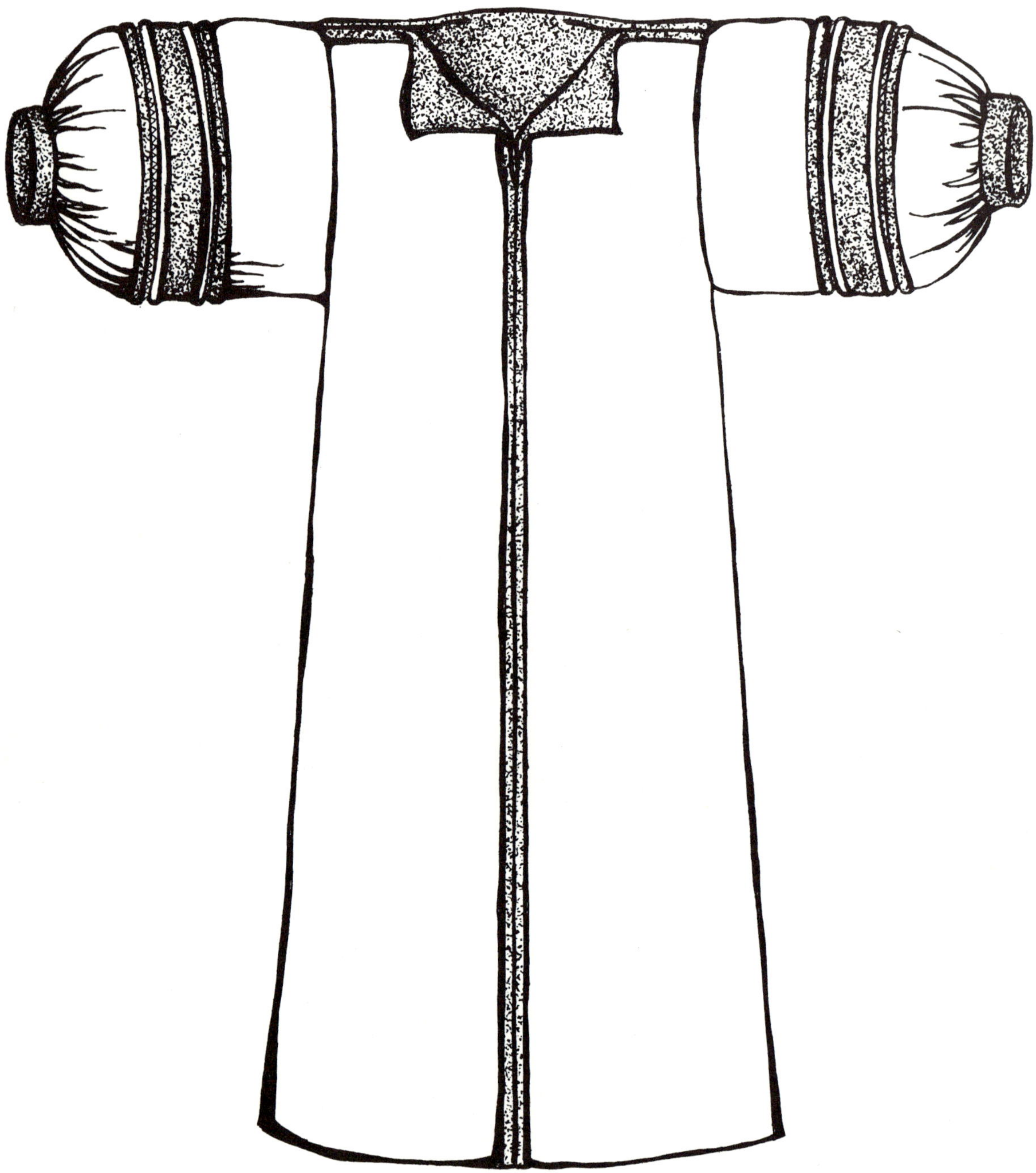

Long dress with insets on sleeves

Making up To make a dark poncho with light hems, use dark side as right side. For a light poncho with dark hems, use light side as right side. Turn and stitch 1.5 cm ($\frac{5}{8}$ in) hems, to wrong side, on all edges of insets. Turn and stitch 1.5 cm ($\frac{5}{8}$ in) hems, to right side, on both short edges, and one long edge of lower hems and main parts. Turn and stitch 5 cm (2 in) hems on remaining edge of main parts, and a 10 cm (4 in) hem on remaining edge of lower hems.

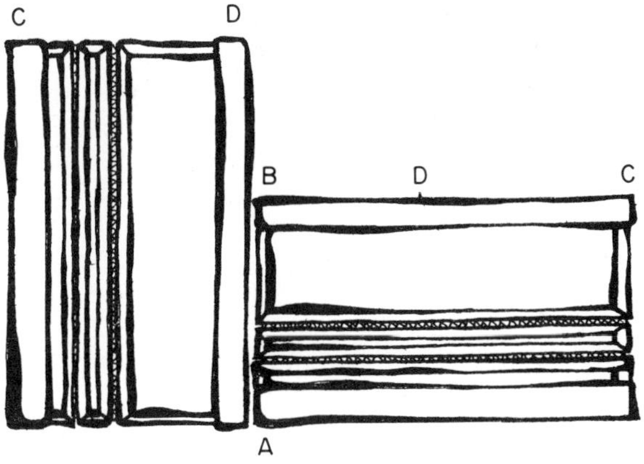

Make back and front up in the same way. With all hems uppermost embroider one edge of inset to narrow hem of upper part. Embroider remaining edge of inset to narrow hem of lower hem. Lay out back and front as shown in diagram above. Embroider seam from A to B, then match C to C, and D to D. Embroider seam from C to D.

Dress

Full length, with wide cuffed sleeves, insets and tie belt. To fit 80–90 cm (32–36 in) bust, length 145 cm (58 in).

Materials 3.7 m ($4\frac{1}{8}$ yd) medium or lightweight denim – after shrinking this should be at least 3.3 m ($3\frac{5}{8}$ yd); thread to match; embroidery thread or threads.

Cutting out Wash and press fabric; then cut into two pieces across width, the first being 180 cm (72 in) long, and the second, 150 cm (60 in) long.

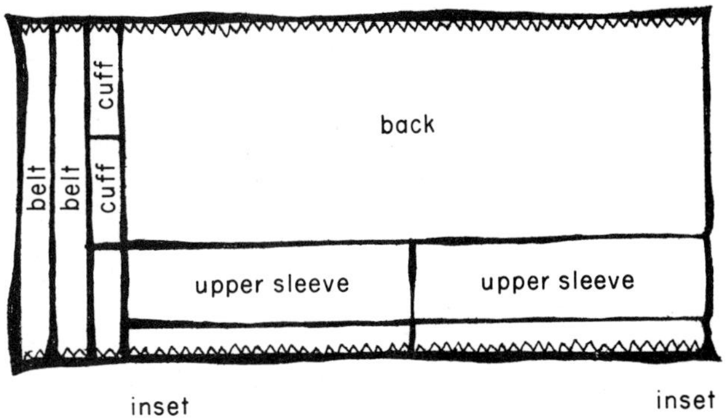

Following the above diagram, from the first piece cut three 10 cm (4 in) strips across fabric. Keep two for the belt. From the third piece cut two cuffs, each 30 cm (12 in) long. Cut a 10 cm (4 in) strip from selvedge of remaining fabric. Cut this in half to give two insets, each 75 cm (30 in) long. Cut a 20 m (8 in) strip parallel to selvedge and cut in half to give two upper sleeves, each 75 cm (30 in) long. This leaves 60 × 150 cm (24 × 60 in) for back.

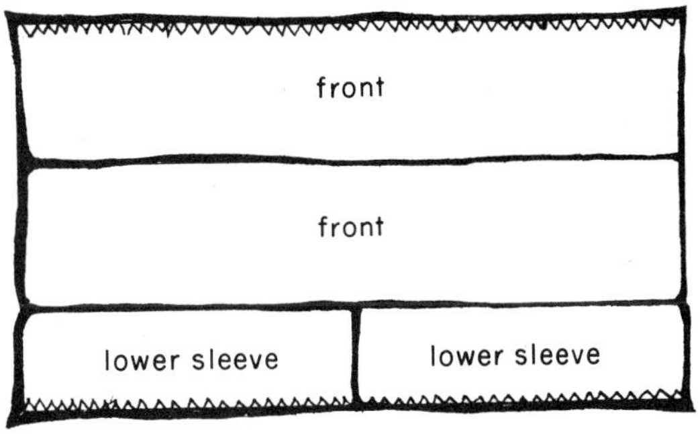

Following the above diagram, and using the second piece of denim, cut two 35 cm (14 in) strips from selvedge for fronts. Cut remaining fabric in half to give two lower sleeves, each 20 × 75 cm (8 × 30 in).

Making up To make a dark dress with light insets, use dark side as right side. For a light dress with dark insets, use light side as right side. Join shorter edges of insets, using run and fell seams. Turn and stitch 1.5 cm ($\frac{5}{8}$ in) hems to wrong side of both long edges. Join shorter edges of lower and upper sleeves, using run and fell seams. Turn and stitch 1.5 cm ($\frac{5}{8}$ in) hem to right side on one long edge of each piece. With all hems uppermost, embroider inset to hem of upper sleeve. Then embroider other edge of inset

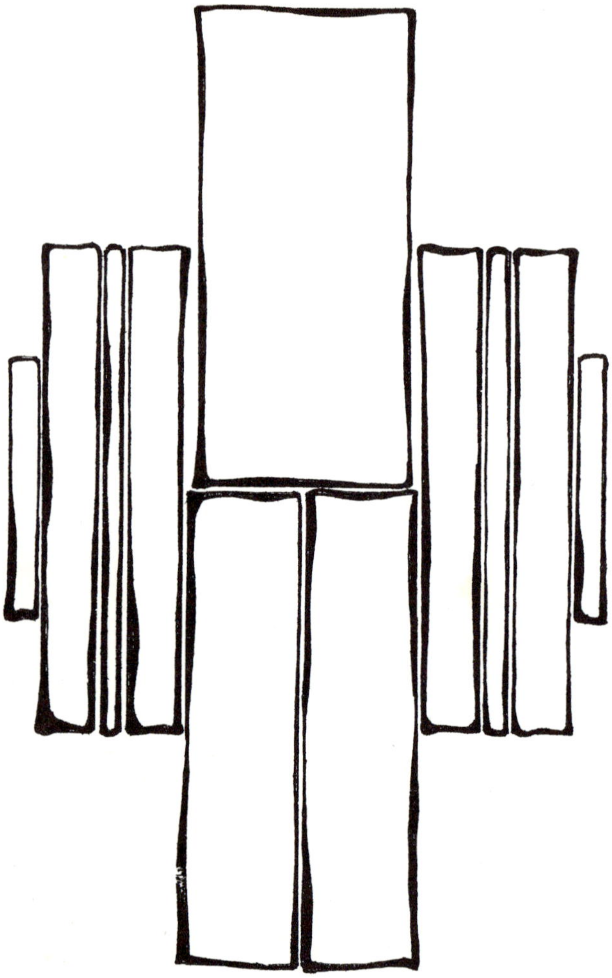

to hem of lower sleeve. With wrong sides together, join shorter edges of cuff with 1.5 cm ($\frac{5}{8}$ in) flat seam. Press. Gather remaining edge of lower sleeve to fit cuff. Place right side of sleeve to wrong side of cuff and make a 1.5 cm ($\frac{5}{8}$ in) flat seam. Press. On remaining edge of cuff, turn and crease 1 cm ($\frac{3}{8}$ in) to wrong side. Fold cuff in half, covering raw edges. Hem into place.

With right sides together sew long edges of front together. Use a 2.5 cm (1 in) flat seam and leave the last 20 cm (8 in) unstitched to form rever. With right sides together place fronts on top of back. Make sure outside edges meet. Then work 2.5 cm (1 in) flat seam, leaving 20 cm (8 in) unstitched at top for neck opening. Press front and shoulder seams open. Turn and stitch 1.5 cm ($\frac{5}{8}$ in) hems on all seam edges, including parts left unstitched for rever and neck opening.

Place centre of remaining edge of upper sleeve to shoulder seam, right sides together. Join sleeve to side seam using 1.5 cm ($\frac{5}{8}$ in) flat seam. Sew second sleeve into place. Join side seam from under arm to bottom edge, right sides together, using a 1.5 cm ($\frac{5}{8}$ in) flat seam. Press seam open.

Try on dress and turn up bottom hem to make dress exact length required. Seam shorter edges of belt together, using 1.5 cm ($\frac{5}{8}$ in) flat seam. Make up as for rouleau. Oversew all raw edges by hand or machine. Press. Fold corners of neck opening to form revers. To make a dress without a belt buy 0.2 m ($\frac{1}{4}$ yd) less denim and ignore instructions for cutting out belt.

EMBROIDERY

Embroidery can be added to any of the things in this book or to ready made clothes. It can be simple, just a few stitches, or complex; it depends more on patience and care than ability.

Choosing your own design

Search through magazines and books for a design that appeals to you. Linear designs are the easiest and most effective. Bear in mind the type of embroidery you intend to use. Unless you have already done a lot of hand embroidery, do not choose a complicated or over-large design. It always takes longer than you think to do and you might find it at the back of a cupboard a year later – still unfinished. Also straight-stitch machine embroidery is difficult to do if the design involves tight curves. Make sure that the design has the right proportions, although its actual size is not important.

Placing design

Try not to place embroidery over seams or anywhere that it will be rubbed. If embroidering before making up, allow for the fabric included in seams and hems. Normally allow about 2.5 cm (1 in) for seams and 3.5 cm ($1\frac{1}{2}$ in) for hems. Mark these lines with chalk and position the design inside them. If embroidering a garment that has already been made up, think carefully about placing embroidery. A sleeve is much more difficult to work on than a cuff. You cannot embroider a sleeve very easily, and it is all too easy to sew through both layers of a sleeve. Similarly with pockets – these are probably best unstitched, embroidered, and then embroidered or topstitched back into place.

Technique

Trace design and enlarge to correct size. See page 21 for enlarging designs. Transfer to the right side of the denim, use carbon. Check that the design is the right way round, especially if you are including any letters. If you are doing a large amount of embroidery, transfer the design to the fabric a bit at a time, as you embroider. Otherwise it will smudge and rub and leave the fabric looking decidedly grubby.

Heavyweight denim can easily be embroidered without a hoop, but it is essential to use a thimble. Many people find that other weights of denim need to be put into an embroidery hoop. This keeps that fabric taut and makes stitching easier. I dislike using an embroidery hoop because I find I am forever having to move the hoop around. Instead I put a piece of iron-on interlining behind the embroidery and bond the fabrics together. This also stops the denim pulling the embroidery stitches when the garment is being worn.

First method – by hand

Equipment Embroidery thread; crewel needles; embroidery hoop or iron-on interlining.

Technique You can work any design using hand embroidery; the limiting factor is the amount of time you have to spend. You will find diagrams showing how to work many embroidery stitches on pages 15–17. For those who are left-handed, I pass on a tip I find invaluable. Prop open the book and place a mirror on the opposite page to the diagram. Adjust the book so that you can see the diagram's reflection. Then work from the reflection. It works equally well for basic sewing diagrams, and layout diagrams, if you find it easier to start cutting at the right-hand side.

The thicker the thread you use the bigger the stitches can be (provided they are not so big that they are easily caught or snagged), and the quicker the work is done. Whatever the thickness of the thread, make sure that the eye of the needle is the right size. If the eye is too small it will be difficult to thread, and when you have succeeded it will fray the thread as you work. Too large an eye and the needle will continually come unthreaded, which is irritating.

It is a false economy to use a long length of thread. By the time you have sorted out the inevitable tangles the thread looks tatty and worn. Use a length which reaches just from the fingers to the elbow, and this will lessen the amount of movement while sewing, and make your arm less tired. If you are sure that the needle suits the thread you are using, but you still find the eye awkward to thread, use a needle threader. (They are often supplied with packets of needles.)

Second method – using a straight-stitch machine
Equipment Sewing thread, the thicker the better; embroidery hoop or iron-on interlining; sewing machine.
Technique This method is most suitable for geometric designs, or designs without tight curves. Contrary to all the 'ads' you do not need a complicated sewing machine to produce beautiful embroidery. Use the thickest machine thread that you can find, or special machine embroidery thread if you can obtain it. Thread up the machine, set it to give a small stitch length, check tension. (This is probably the only time I recommend a small stitch, but, as the machine then stitches quite slowly you have more time to manoeuvre the denim, so it is easier to do.)

If you use a hoop for this particular form of embroidery you will find that you have to move it frequently – interlining the denim is easier. Stitch carefully along the lines of the design. When turning corners make sure that the needle is through the fabric, raise presser foot and turn the denim, without pulling the needle. Lower presser foot and carry on sewing. Go over the design lines several times for a bolder effect. It is easier to let the lines of stitching cross back and forth than to try and keep them parallel. Any mistakes or straying from the line then look intentional. Be sure to fasten all ends of threads securely on the wrong side.

Third method – using a swing needle machine
Equipment Sewing thread; embroidery hoop or iron-on interfacing; swing needle machine.
Technique You can use this method for most designs. Since the denim moves very slowly you have a great deal of control. It is quite quick to do, but takes a lot of thread.

Machine satin stitch is very easy to do. You can use ordinary sewing thread or machine embroidery thread. Thread machine and adjust stitch length to its minimum, so that the stitches are almost on top of each other, but the denim still moves through very slowly. Set the swing of the needle. Check tension. Stitch along lines of design. You should produce a band of satin stitch. If it is too open, adjust length of stitch. If it is uneven go over it again.

By altering the swing of the needle you alter the width of the band of embroidery. By changing the swing as you sew you can produce graduated bands. If you are undertaking a considerable amount of this type of embroidery do allow your machine to cool down now and then. Experiment with the different methods of embroidery and find which suits you best.

Embroidered clutch bag

This will be approximately 30 × 15 cm (12 × 6 in).
Materials 0.35 m ($\frac{3}{8}$ yd) of any weight denim; thread to match; embroidery thread or threads; 0.3 m ($\frac{3}{8}$ yd) iron-on interlining (optional).
Cutting out Cut denim between selvedges to give a piece 35 × 47.5 cm (19 × 13$\frac{1}{2}$ in) for lining. From remaining piece cut a 5 cm (2 in) strip from width to leave a piece 30 × 42.5 cm (17 × 11$\frac{1}{2}$ in) for main part.

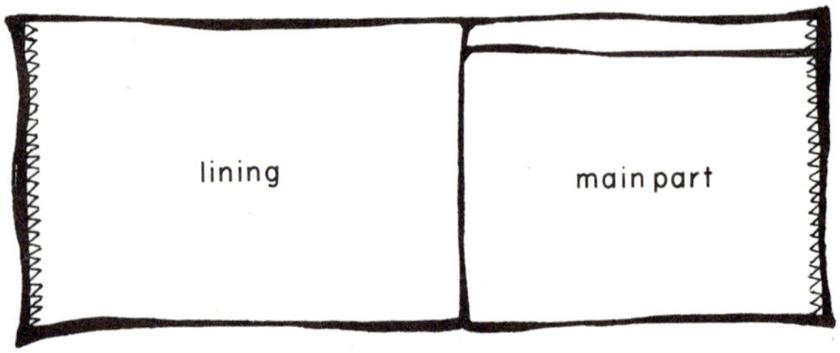

Making up To make a dark bag with light edges, use dark side as right side. For a light bag with dark edges, use light side as right side.

Embroidered clutch bags

If used, bond interlining to wrong side of main part using a hot iron. Using chalk, mark 5 cm (2 in) margin on both long sides and one short side of main part. Enlarge design to fit this. (You could use the design from the tunic.)

Transfer design to right side of denim and work embroidery. When finished, place wrong side of main part to right side of lining, leaving 2.5 cm (1 in) of lining showing all round. Tack together, then make edges of lining into 1.5 cm ($\frac{5}{8}$ in) hems to cover raw edges of main part. Stitch into place. Fold up bottom 15 cm (6 in) to form pocket. Oversew side edges. Fold flap over.

Embroidered tunic in three sizes

A versatile garment that can be worn over jeans and a jersey, or over a dress. With or without its tie belt. In three sizes to fit from 65–105 cm (26–42 in) chest or bust.

Large
To fit 95–105 cm (38–42 in) chest or bust, length 75 cm (30 in).
Materials 1.8 m (2 yd) medium or heavy-weight denim – this should measure at least 1.6 m ($1\frac{3}{4}$ yd) after shrinking; thread to match; thread for embroidery.
Cutting out Wash and press denim, cut two 10 cm (4 in) strips across the width of denim for belt. Cut remaining denim in half across width to give two pieces, each 70 × 90 cm (27 × 36 in) for back and front.

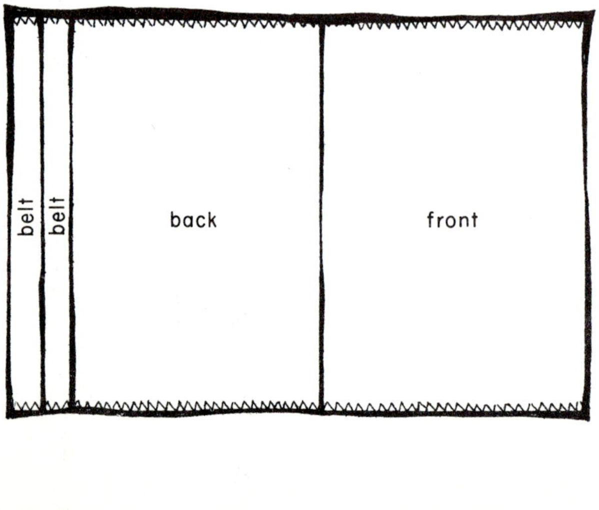

Making up To make a light tunic with dark edging, use light side as right side. For a dark tunic, with light edging, use dark side as right side.

On the right side of front, mark 5 cm (2 in) margins on both long sides, and a 15 cm (6 in) margin on one short side (bottom edge). Trace the above diagram and enlarge to fit. Transfer to right side of denim. Work embroidery. Press. Embroider back in the same way.

With wrong sides together, work 2.5 cm (1 in) flat seam across the top edge. Leave 35 cm (14 in) unstitched at centre for head opening. Work 2.5 cm (1 in) flat seams down sides, wrong sides together. Leave 30 cm (12 in) unstitched at top and bottom of seam for armholes and side slits. Press seams open along their entire length. Turn and stitch seams to make 1.5 cm ($\frac{5}{8}$ in) hems. Turn and stitch 5 cm (2 in) hems on bottom edges of back and front. Join short edges of belt and make up as for rouleau.
To adjust length To shorten or lengthen tunic alter the width of bottom hem – you will also have to alter the position of the embroidery. To make a tunic without a belt, buy 0.2 m ($\frac{1}{4}$ yd) less denim and omit cutting instructions for belt.

Medium
To fit 80–90 cm (32–36 in) chest or bust, length 75 cm (30 in).
Materials 1.6 m ($1\frac{7}{8}$ yd) medium or heavy-weight denim – this should measure at least 1.4 m ($1\frac{5}{8}$ yd) after shrinking; thread to match; thread for embroidery.
Cutting out Wash and press denim. Then, following diagram for cutting out large tunic, cut two 10 cm (4 in) strips across width of denim for belt. Cut remaining denim in half across width to give two pieces, each 60 × 90 cm (24 × 36 in) for back and front.
Making up Make up as for large tunic, but leave only 32.5 cm (13 in) for head opening.

Embroidered tunic

Small

To fit 65–75 cm (26–30 in) chest, length 55 cm (22 in).

Materials 0.9 m (1 yd) medium or heavyweight denim – this should measure at least 0.8 m ($\frac{7}{8}$ yd) after shrinking; thread to match; thread for embroidery.

Cutting out Wash and press denim. Then following diagram for cutting out large tunic, cut two 7.5 cm (3 in) strips across width of fabric for belt. Cut remaining fabric in half between selvedges to give two pieces, each 45 × 65 cm (18 × 25 in) for back and front.

Making up Make up as for large tunic, but leave 30 cm (12 in) for head opening, and 20 cm (8 in) for armholes and side slits.

Embroidered dress in three sizes

Can be worn as a summer dress or as a pinafore. It comes in three sizes. To fit 80–95 cm (32–38 in) bust, length 105 cm (42 in).

Materials 3 m (3$\frac{3}{8}$ yd) of medium or lightweight denim – this should be at least 2.65 m (3$\frac{7}{8}$ yd) after shrinking; thread to match; thread for embroidery; curtain rings.

Cutting out Wash and press denim. Then cut across width of denim to give two pieces, each 75 × 90 cm (30 × 36 in) for back and front.

Mark armholes 10 cm (4 in) from corner on one long side, and from the same corner mark 5 cm (2 in) on shorter side. Join these marks with a curved line and cut off corner. Place shorter edges together and cut second armhole to match. Then cut three 30 cm (12 in) strips for frill. From remaining fabric cut two 5 cm (2 in) strips. Cut these in half to give four straps, each 5 × 45 cm (2 × 18 in). This leaves 15 × 90 cm (6 × 36 in).

For bust 80 cm (32 in) cut four pieces, each 7.5 × 27.5 cm (3 × 11 in) for yokes. For bust 85 cm (34 in) cut four pieces, each 7.5 × 30 cm (3 × 12 in) for yokes. For bust 90 cm (36 in) cut four pieces, each 7.5 × 32.5 cm (3 × 13 in) for yokes. For bust 95 cm (38 in) cut four pieces, each 7.5 × 35 cm (3 × 14 in) for yokes.

Making up To make a dark dress with light yoke and hem, use dark side as right side. For a light dress with dark yoke and hem, use light side as right side. On right side of three pieces for frill mark 15 cm (6 in) margin on one long side, and 3 cm (1$\frac{1}{4}$ in) on both short edges. Trace the two diagrams below. (They are actual size.) Arrange motifs alternately 5 cm (2 in) apart along frills. Transfer one motif at a time to avoid them smudging as you work.

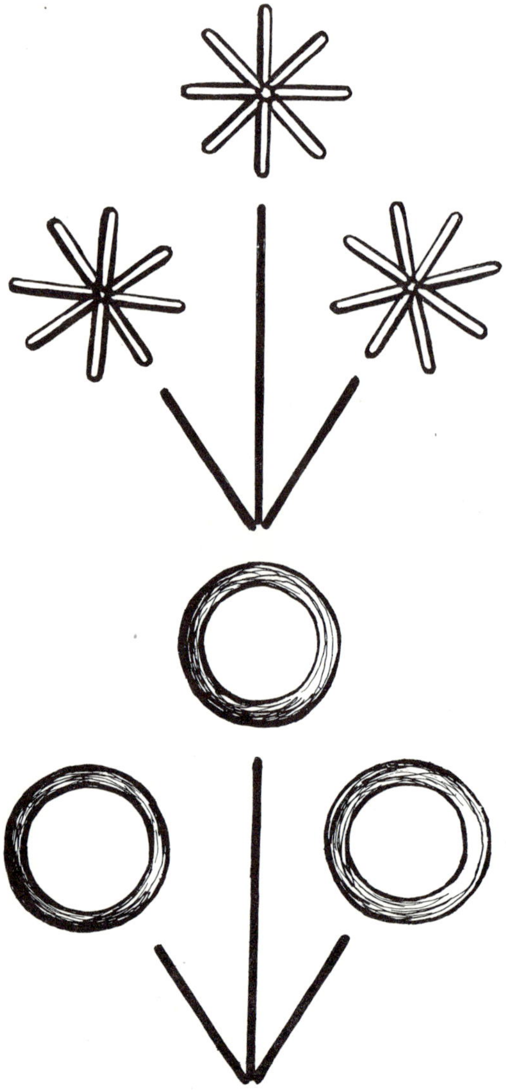

Embroidered dress

Work embroidery and attach rings. Brass curtain rings are the most suitable. They will not rust – but try not to leave any garment decorated with metal rings soaking in water. If you cannot buy brass rings, use plastic curtain rings. Either type of ring can be covered by working closed buttonhole stitch around it, as for an eyelet. In this way you can add extra colour or match the colour of the denim. Attach rings to denim by oversewing at intervals.

Join short edges of frill using run and fell seams. Be careful that you do not get any of the pieces twisted. Turn and stitch 5 cm (2 in) hem on bottom edge of frill. Join side seams of back and front using run and fell seams. Turn 1 cm ($\frac{3}{8}$ in) hem to wrong side on armhole edge. Gather frill to fit bottom edge of back and front, right sides together. Sew using a 1.5 cm ($\frac{5}{8}$ in) flat seam.

On wrong side of two yoke pieces, one for back, one for front, mark 2.5 cm ($1\frac{1}{2}$ in) margins on all edges. Within these lines embroider three stars and attach two rings. Gather top edge of front so that it is 3 cm ($1\frac{1}{4}$ in) shorter than longer side of yoke. Place embroidered side of yoke against right side of front, leaving 1.5 cm ($\frac{5}{8}$ in) of yoke extending each side. Sew using 1.5 cm ($\frac{5}{8}$ in) flat seam.

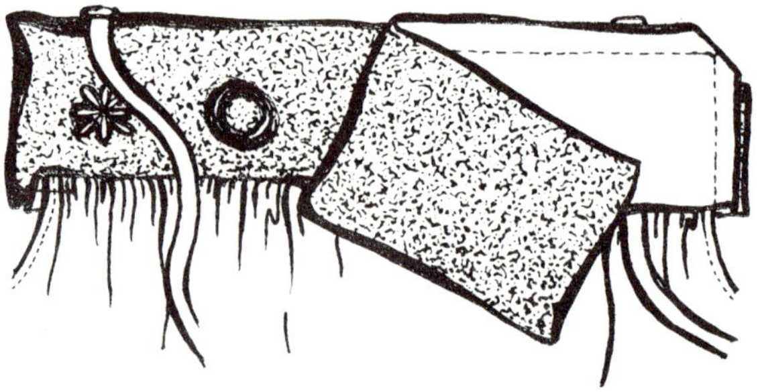

Make ties into rouleau and sew to remaining long edge of yoke, 5 cm (2 in) from corners, as in diagram above. Place second, unembroidered, yoke on top; sew 1.5 cm ($\frac{5}{8}$ in) flat seam on top and side edges. Trim corners and turn right side out. Turn under 1.5 cm ($\frac{5}{8}$ in) on remaining long edge. Hem into place to cover raw edges.

Attach back yoke in the same way. Oversew raw edges of frill by hand or by machine. Press.

PATCHWORK

Patchwork is one of the oldest traditional crafts. Examples have been found that were worked two thousand years ago. It is based on geometric shapes which can be joined endlessly to make a larger area of patterned fabric.

Block patchwork

One simple form of patchwork is derived from traditional American block quilts. As patterns are built up from simple shapes there is no need to mount the pieces on backing papers – which takes ages. The patterns can all be machine sewn – saving still more time, so making a patchwork bedcover no longer the labour of years. Throughout this section, 'patch' means the shape to be joined and 'block' refers to the pattern made by the joined patches.

To make templates Patterns for templates can be made in two ways. The first method is better suited to patterns such as Pinwheel, where the block is quartered. The second method is better suited to patterns such as Nine Patch, where (as the name implies) the block is divided into nine sections.

First method You will need household scissors and paper. Cut paper to the exact size of the finished block. Make sure that the corners are right-angled. Fold the paper in half, then fold in half again, making sure that the edges meet exactly. Unfold the paper.

Now fold corner to corner to give diagonal creases, and fold again if necessary. Cut one example of each shape.

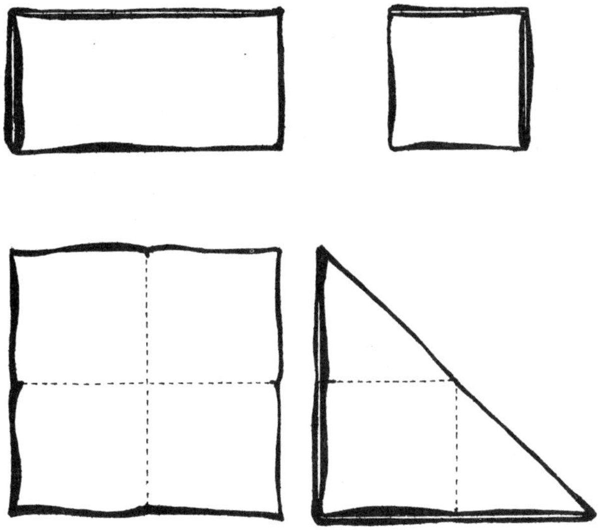

Second method For this method you will need paper, household scissors, a set square and a ruler. Cut paper to the exact size of the finished block. Make sure that the corners are right-angled. Measure length of side, divide by three, use set square and ruler to divide block into nine patches. Use ruler to draw in diagonals. Cut out one example of each shape.

Once you have your paper patterns use them to cut card templates. This gives you a template the exact size of the patch, without seam allowances. Cut templates as accurately as possible, using a knife and straight edge. If you find the second method difficult, there is no reason why you should not use the first method to make a block based on nine patches, but you will have to be very careful when folding the paper into three. Similarly you can make a quartered patch by the second method if preferred.

Technique Place templates on fabric, making sure that they are parallel to the selvedge. (If the grain of the fabric runs across the straight edge of a patch it will stretch and be difficult to sew.) Allow 1.5 cm ($\frac{5}{8}$ in) all round each template for seam allowance, i.e. 3 cm ($1\frac{1}{4}$ in) between templates. Draw round each template and cut out to include seam allowance. Join patches with 1.5 cm ($\frac{5}{8}$ in) flat seams, using chalk lines as sewing guide. Fasten all threads securely. If you wish you can cut templates to include the 1.5 cm ($\frac{5}{8}$ in) seam allowance, and place them next to each other when cutting out, but you will not have any guide lines for sewing. Since denim has two distinctive sides you can cut all the patches from one piece of fabric and then arrange them dark side or light side up as needed.

Block patterns

Pinwheel Cut one triangular template. Using this, cut eight denim triangles for each block. Following the diagram, join dark and light triangles in pairs along their longest edges. Be careful not to stretch this diagonal seam. Press. Join resultant triangles so that the points of triangles meet at the centre. Press.

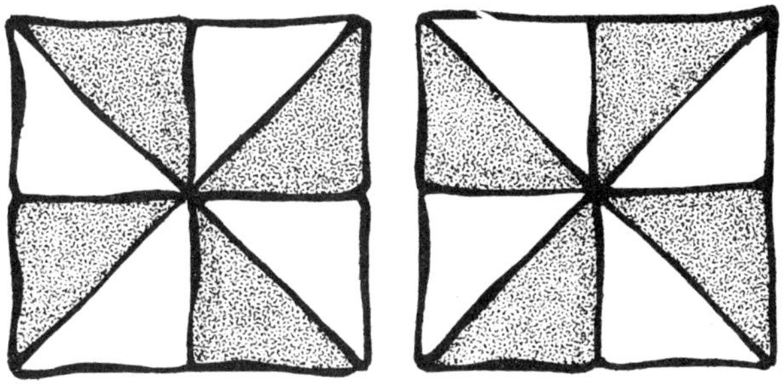

Windmill This is a variant of Pinwheel. Cut one large and one small triangular template. Using these cut four large and eight small denim triangles for each block. Following the diagram, join small, dark and light triangles in pairs along their straight edges. Press. Join each resultant triangle to a large triangle along their longest edges. Then join as for Pinwheel.

Nine Patch Cut one square template. Using this, cut nine denim squares for each block. Following the diagram, take squares needed for top line. Arrange as shown and seam together. Press. Arrange and make up second and third lines in the same way. Arrange three completed strips and seam first and second, second and third strips together. Make sure the corners of patches match. Press.

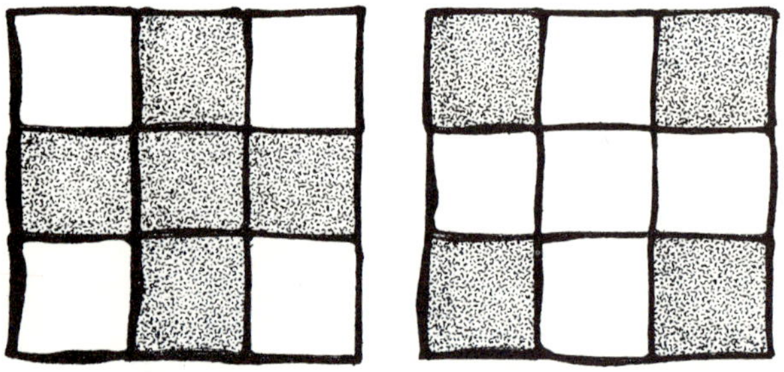

Whirlwind Cut one square and one triangular template. Using these, cut five denim squares and eight denim triangles for each block. Join light and dark triangles in pairs along their longest edge, being careful not to stretch this seam. Press. Arrange and join resultant patches as for Nine Patch.

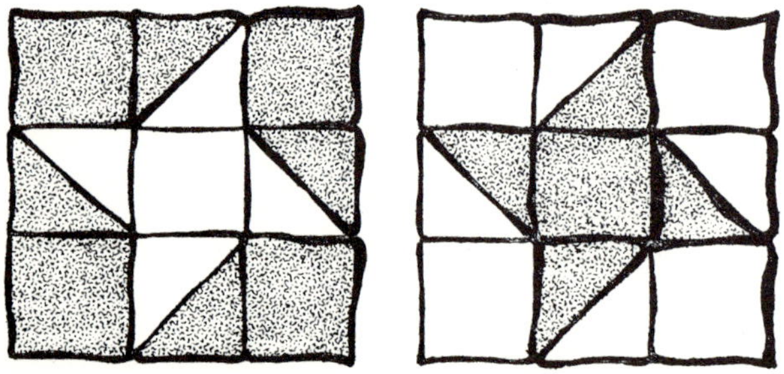

Shoo Fly Cut one square and one triangular template. Using these, cut five squares and eight triangles from denim. Make up as for Whirlwind.

This is a variant of Shoo Fly and is made up in exactly the same way.

Churn Dash This is another, rather more complicated variant of Shoo Fly, and resembles an ancient implement called a churn dash. Cut one square, one rectangular and one triangular template. Using these cut one denim square, eight denim rectangles and eight denim triangles. Join light and dark rectangles in pairs along their longer edges. Press. Then follow instructions for Shoo Fly.

Bear's Paw Cut one square and one triangular template. Using these, cut three denim squares and ten denim triangles for each block. Join as shown in the diagram.

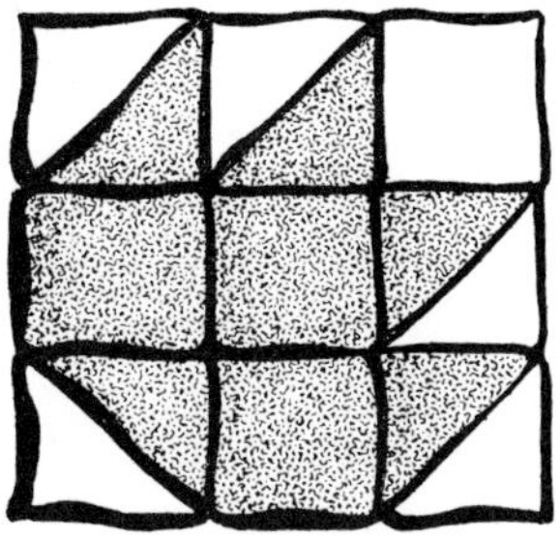

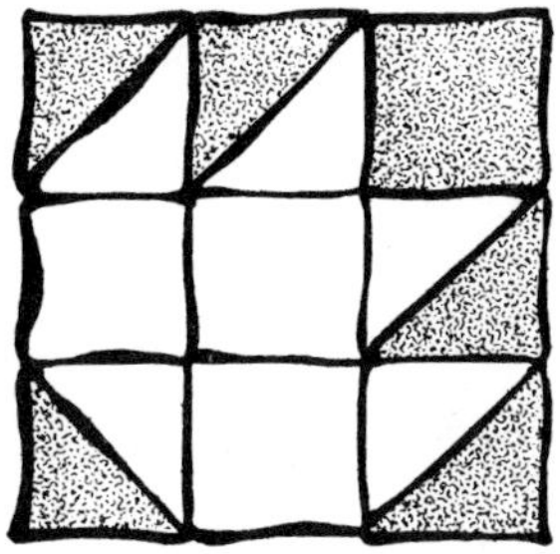

Maple Leaf This is made in the same way as Bear's Paw. After the final pressing the stem is embroidered.

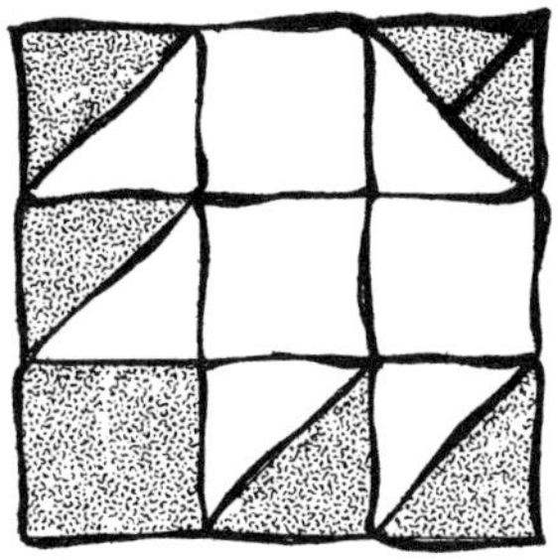

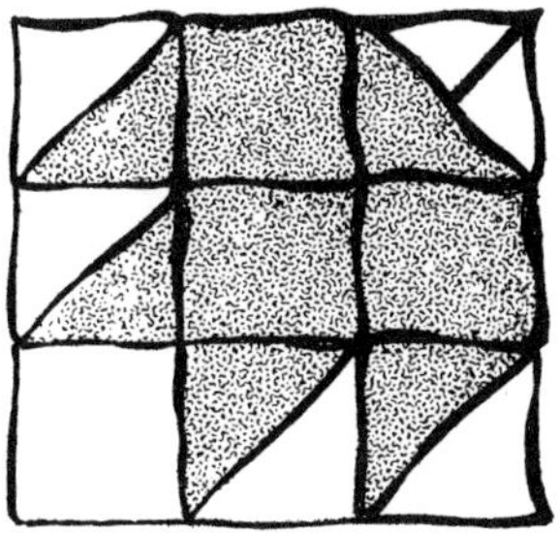

Denim patchwork can be used for clothes but is more easily adapted for use as household furnishing. Nowadays denim comes in a range of colours, not just blue – so choose a colour to fit in with your home.

Small cushion

This is to fit a cushion pad between 30 cm (12 in) and 46 cm (18 in) square. A cushion of this size is best made with one block the same size as the pad – but this can be done in four ways. You can use the same block on each side – neat and tidy. Or you can use the same block, but reverse the colours – a subtle difference. Thirdly, you could use different blocks for each side – and turn the cushion over when you fancy a change. Finally, you can make onc side of the cushion plain. This takes less denim, and less time.

Materials 0.9 m (1 yd) of any weight denim – this should be at least 0.8 m ($\frac{7}{8}$ yd) after shrinking; thread to match; cushion pad.

Cutting out Wash and press denim. Measure cushion. Then choose one of the blocks given and make up templates to fit cushion. Use templates to cut out enough patches for two blocks.

Making up Make up blocks using 1.5 cm ($\frac{5}{8}$ in) flat seams. Press. Put back and front together, right side to right side. Sew 1.5 cm ($\frac{5}{8}$ in) flat seam on three sides and just round corners of fourth side. Turn right side out and insert cushion pad. Oversew opening.

To make a cushion with a plain back you will only need 0.8 m ($\frac{7}{8}$ yd) of denim, which will be at least 0.7 m ($\frac{3}{4}$ yd) after shrinking. Wash and press denim. Then cut plain block for back, adding 1.5 cm ($\frac{5}{8}$ in) seam allowance on all edges. Cut enough patches for one block. Make up one block, then join back and front as above.

Floor cushions

Large floor cushions can be made up in many ways. I give instructions for four – and ideas for many others. They are for a 90 cm (36 in) cushion pad.

Nine Patch cushion

Materials 3.1 m ($3\frac{3}{8}$ yd) of any weight denim – this should be at least 2.8 m (3 yd) after shrinking; thread to match; 90 cm (36 in) square cushion pad.

Cutting out Wash and press denim. Then cut sixteen 33 cm ($13\frac{1}{4}$ in) squares, and eighteen 13 cm ($5\frac{1}{4}$ in) squares.

Making up Join nine small squares as for Nine Patch. Press. Use this finished block as the centre square of a larger block made from eight large squares. Make up second complete block; be sure that the two sides are reversed. Complete as for small cushion.

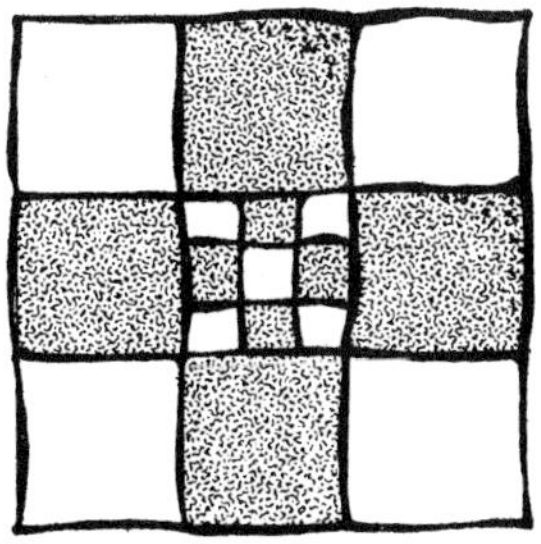

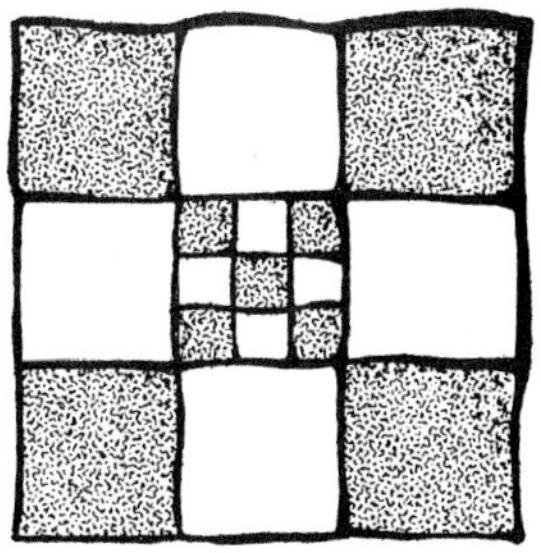

a

b

Floor cushions: a) Nine Patch b) Pinwheel c) Maple Leaf d) Whirlwind

c

d

Pinwheel cushion
Materials 3.1 m (3⅜ yd) of any weight denim – this should be at least 2.8 m (3 yd) after shrinking; thread to match; 90 cm (36 in) square cushion pad.

Cutting out Wash and press denim. To make templates for triangles, fold a 15 cm (6 in) square of paper in half diagonally. From denim cut nine 33 cm (13¼ in) squares. Cut seventy-two triangles from template, remember to include 1.5 cm (⅝ in) seam allowance on all edges.
Making up Join triangles to make nine Pinwheel blocks. Then join these blocks to large squares, using the diagram as a guide. Join completed back and front as for small cushion.

Maple Leaf cushion
Materials 3.1 m (3⅜ yd) of any weight denim – this should be at least 2.8 m (3 yd) after shrinking; thread to match; thread for embroidery; 90 cm (36 in) square cushion pad.
Cutting out Wash and press denim. To make templates for triangles, fold a 15 cm (6 in) square of paper in half diagonally. From denim cut

thirty-two 18.5 cm (7¼ in) squares. Then cut 160 triangles; remember to include 1.5 cm (⅝ in) seam allowances on all edges.
Making up Following the diagram, make up eight blocks. Four for each side. Embroider stems. Join blocks together with stems at centre. Complete as for small cushion.

Whirlwind cushion
Materials 3.1 m (3⅜ yd) of any weight denim – this should be at least 2.8 m (3 yd) after shrinking; thread to match; 90 cm (36 in) square cushion pad.

Cutting out Wash and press denim. To make a template for triangles, fold a 10 cm (4 in) square of paper diagonally. From denim cut eight 33 cm (13¼ in) squares and fifty 13 cm (5¼ in) squares. Then cut eight triangles, remembering to add 1.5 cm (⅝ in) seam allowance on all edges.
Making up Make small squares and triangles into nine Whirlwind blocks. Then following the diagram, join these with large squares to give back and front of cushion. Complete as for small cushion.

Designing your own cushions
Measure your cushion pad and work out how many blocks you will need and their size. For instance a square cushion can be made from one block (see small cushions), from four blocks (see Maple Leaf floor cushion), from nine blocks, or from sixteen blocks. For an oblong cushion you might have to add plain strips, or extra squares.

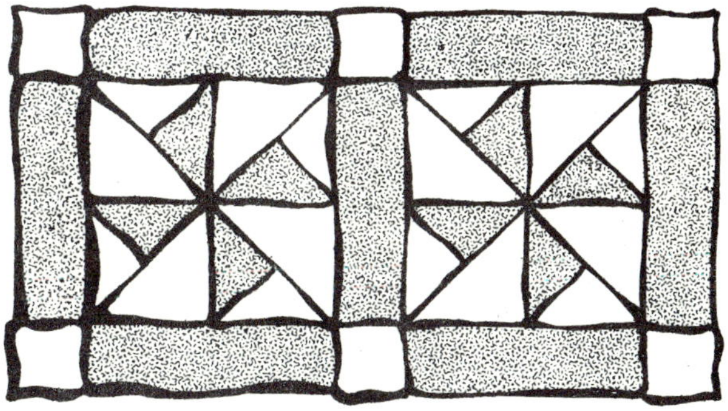

You can use one block as an all over pattern (see Maple Leaf floor cushion) or patchwork blocks alternated with plain blocks (see Pinwheel and Whirlwind floor cushions). Variants of the same block look good together (see Shoo Fly and Churn Dash used on bedspread). Work out your design on squared paper and count how many of each shape you will need. (Remember that you will need a back and a front.) Cut templates and arrange on paper, including seam allowance, to find out how much denim you will need. Add approximately ten per cent extra fabric for shrinking.

Bedspread in two sizes

You need space to spread out and patience, not skill, to make such a large article. If the number of patches needed daunts you, rope in family and friends to help cut them out and piece them together.

Single bedspread
This will be approximately 190 × 250 cm (76 × 100 in) when finished.
Materials 11 m ($12\frac{1}{2}$ yd) of any weight denim – which will be at least 10 m ($11\frac{1}{4}$ yd) after shrinking; 5.5 m ($6\frac{1}{4}$ yd) cotton lining 90 cm (36 in) wide – after shrinking this should be at least 5 m ($5\frac{3}{4}$ yd); 5 m ($5\frac{3}{4}$ yd) 65 gr (2 oz) washable quilting fabric, 90 cm (36 in) wide (optional); thread to match.
Cutting out Wash and press denim. You will find this easier if you cut it into two lengths. Wash and press cotton lining – or you can use an old sheet, which will not have to be shrunk as it has already been washed. Cut lining into two 25 cm (100 in) lengths across width of fabric. If used, cut quilting fabric into two 250 cm (100 in) lengths.

From selvedge of denim cut two 10 cm (4 in) strips, each 275 cm (110 in) long, and two 10 cm (4 in) strips, each 190 cm (76 in) long. Then cut fifty-two 23 cm ($9\frac{1}{4}$ in) squares. Fold a 20 cm (8 in) square in half diagonally to make template for triangles. Cut 96 triangles; remember to add 1.5 cm ($\frac{5}{8}$ in) seam allowance on all edges. Fold second 20 cm (8 in) square in half for rectangular template. Cut sixteen rectangles, including 1.5 cm ($\frac{5}{8}$ in) seam allowance.
Making up Using illustration of single bedspread as a guide, make up blocks. You will have four Shoo Fly blocks, two Churn Dash blocks and six blocks that are a variant of Shoo Fly. Join blocks together as shown, and press thoroughly. Sew strips to edges of patchwork, mitring corners. Sew long edges of lining together, using a 1.5 cm ($\frac{5}{8}$ in) seam. If used, tack quilting fabric to the wrong side of the patchwork. To make sure that it is held firmly, tack it to the corners of each block. Place right side of patchwork and right side of lining together. Sew 1.5 cm ($\frac{5}{8}$ in) flat seam on all four edges, leaving a gap big enough to turn the spread through. Turn to right side and oversew opening.

Double bedspread
This will be approximately 250 cm (100 in) square.
Materials 16.5 m ($18\frac{1}{4}$ yd) of any weight denim – after shrinking this should be at least 15 m ($16\frac{1}{4}$ yd); 8.3 m ($9\frac{1}{2}$ yd) of cotton lining, 90 cm (36 in) wide – after shrinking this should be at least 7.5 m ($8\frac{3}{8}$ yd); 7.5 m ($8\frac{3}{8}$ yd) 65 gr (2 oz) washable quilting fabric, 90 cm (36 in) wide; thread to match.
Cutting out Wash and press denim. You will find this easier if you cut the denim into three lengths. Wash and press cotton lining – or you can use an old double sheet, which will not have to be shrunk as it has already been washed. Cut lining into three 250 cm (100 in) lengths across widths of fabric. If used, cut quilting fabric into three 250 cm (100 in) lengths.

From selvedge of denim cut four 10 cm (4 in) strips, each 275 cm (110 in) long. Then cut sixty-four 23 cm ($9\frac{1}{4}$ in) squares. Fold a 20 cm (8 in) square of paper in half diagonally to make template for triangles. Cut 128 triangles, remembering to add 1.5 cm ($\frac{5}{8}$ in) seam allowance on all edges. Fold a second 20 cm (8 in) square in half to make rectangular template. Cut thirty-two rectangles, including 1.5 cm ($\frac{5}{8}$ in) seam allowance.
Making up Use illustration of double bedspread as a guide, and make up four Shoo Fly blocks, four Churn Dash blocks and eight blocks that are a variant of Shoo Fly. Then make up as for single bedspread.

Designing your own bedspread
I find patchwork quilts fascinating in their variety. Made up as bedspreads, without the quilting, they are not too time consuming and can be just as original. For a start there are many

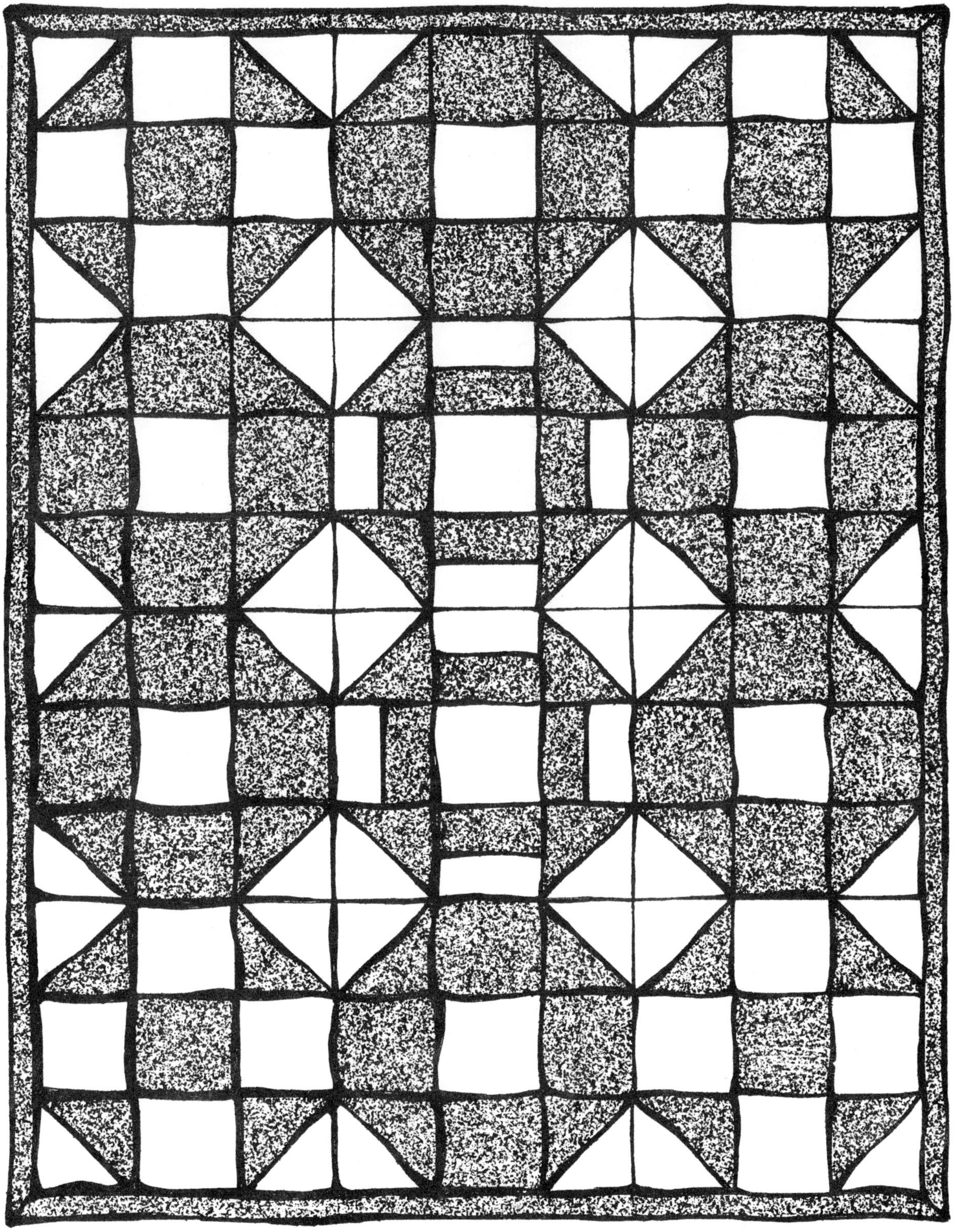

Single bedspread

Double bedspread

ways of arranging the blocks. A single spread can be made from twelve 60 cm (24 in) blocks, arranged in four rows of three, or from forty-eight 30 cm (12 in) blocks, arranged in eight rows of six. A double spread can be made from four 120 cm (48 in) blocks, or from nine 80 cm (32 in) blocks. From sixteen 60 cm (24 in) blocks, arranged in four rows of four, or from sixty-four 30 cm (12 in) blocks, arranged in eight rows of eight. You can alternate patchwork and plain blocks, use all patchwork blocks, or different patchwork blocks. The list of possibilities is endless.

Plan out your own spread on squared paper; there is nothing to stop you planning your own patchwork blocks, or variants of the ones given (but if you then look in a book of patchwork you will probably find that someone else thought of it first). Other nice touches are to embroider some of the plain blocks, or the centre of patchwork blocks. Add your initials and date of working to your future family heirloom. You could make patchwork spreads for cots, bunk beds or extra large luxury beds. Or you might make a bedroom rug (backed with an old blanket), or a headboard cover; there are hundreds of possibilities.

Hand patchwork

This second form of patchwork demands careful cutting and preparation for good results. It is true to say that more time is spent in preparing patches than in sewing. So although it can be used in the same way as block patchwork, its use is normally limited by the patience of the worker.

Equipment

Basic sewing equipment
tracing paper
soft pencil
ball-point pen
thick card
knife and straight edge
cartridge or wrapping paper
household scissors

Technique Trace template. Turn tracing paper over and scribble over lines with a soft pencil. Turn right side up and place on thick card. Then go over the lines of the tracing with a ball-point pen using a ruler or straight edge as a guide. (The pencil on the back will act as carbon paper.)

Cut out template, using knife and straight edge. (If you intend to do a large amount of patchwork cut templates from plywood, plastic or sheet metal.) Draw round template onto paper, and then cut out using household scissors. (So long as the paper is fairly thick and stiff you can use old envelopes, christmas cards or packaging material.) This is your backing shape. Cut one for each patch. Draw round template onto denim, and cut out leaving a 1 cm ($\frac{3}{8}$ in) margin all round for seam allowance. Where two shapes touch you will have to leave 2 cm ($\frac{3}{4}$ in) between them. Cut out correct number of patches, arranging shapes as for finished patchwork to avoid waste. Sort patches into those that are to be dark and those that are to be light.

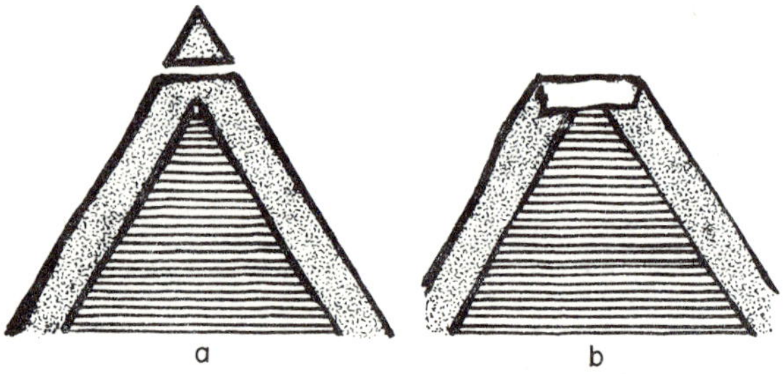

a) Place the backing shape centrally on wrong side of patch. Trim corners if necessary.
b) Fold the corners over the backing shape.

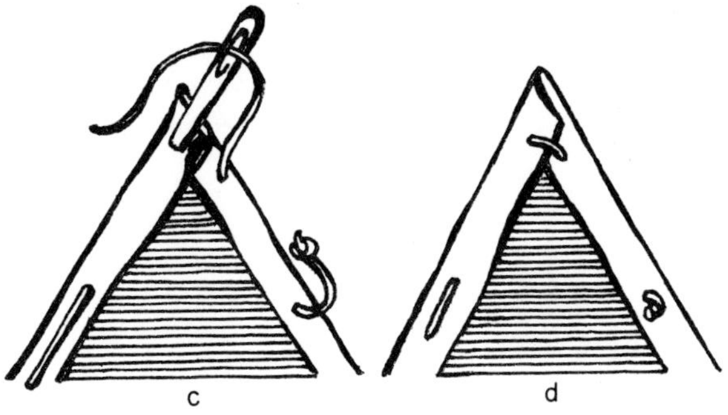

c) Fold edges over backing shape and crease into place.

d) Tack in place, taking special care over corners.

Mount all the shapes in the same way. Preparing the patches does take more time than sewing them together. It is the sort of thing you can do whilst watching television or listening to the radio; for a large piece of patchwork you cannot beat a sewing bee, where friends and relations sew whilst they natter.

Arrange mounted patches as for final pattern. Oversew adjoining edges. Be sure to fasten all the ends firmly. (To misquote: patchwork is only as firm as its weakest stitch.) When all the patches are sewn together, press well and remove tacking and backing papers.

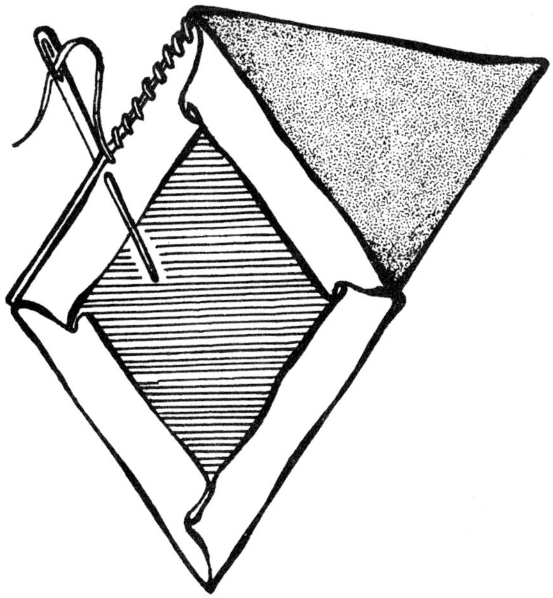

Patchwork handbag

This will be approximately 30 × 20 cm (12 × 8 in) when completed.

Materials 0.8 m ($\frac{7}{8}$ yd) of any weight denim – this should be at least 0.7 m ($\frac{3}{4}$ yd) after shrinking; two pieces of heavy card 30 × 5 cm (12 × 2 in); 0.35 m ($\frac{1}{2}$ yd) interlining (optional).

Cutting out Following the diagram, cut a 33 cm (13 in) strip across the width of the denim.

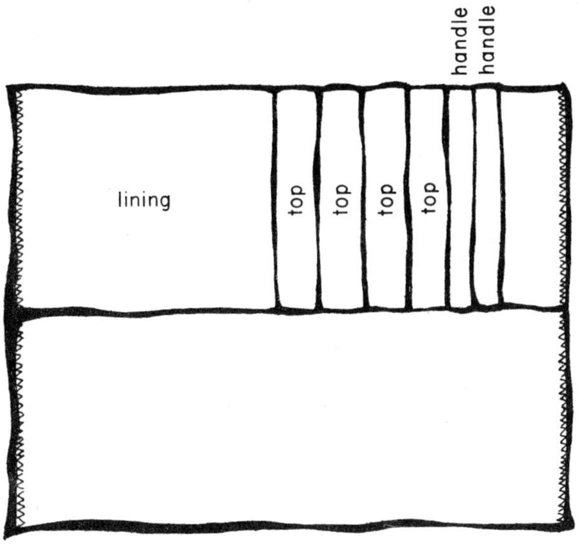

From this cut 40 × 33 cm (16 × 13 in) for bag lining. Then cut four pieces, each 33 × 8 cm (13 × 3 in) for top of bag, and two pieces, each 33 × 5 cm (13 × 2 in) for handles and leaving 33 × 10 cm (13 × 4 in). Use this piece and remaining fabric for patches.

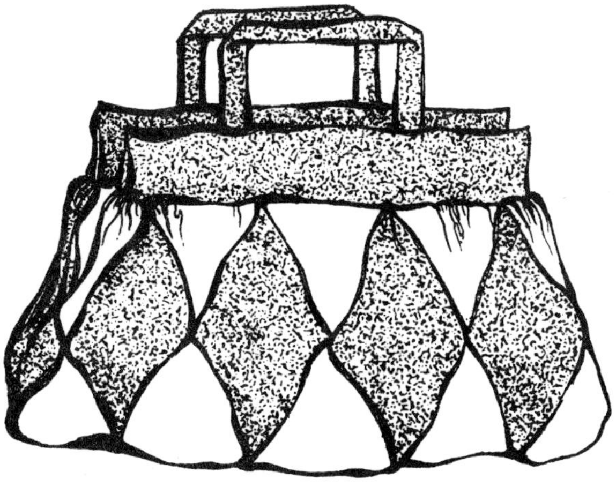

Trace the following diagram and use to make a template. Then cut thirteen whole patches.

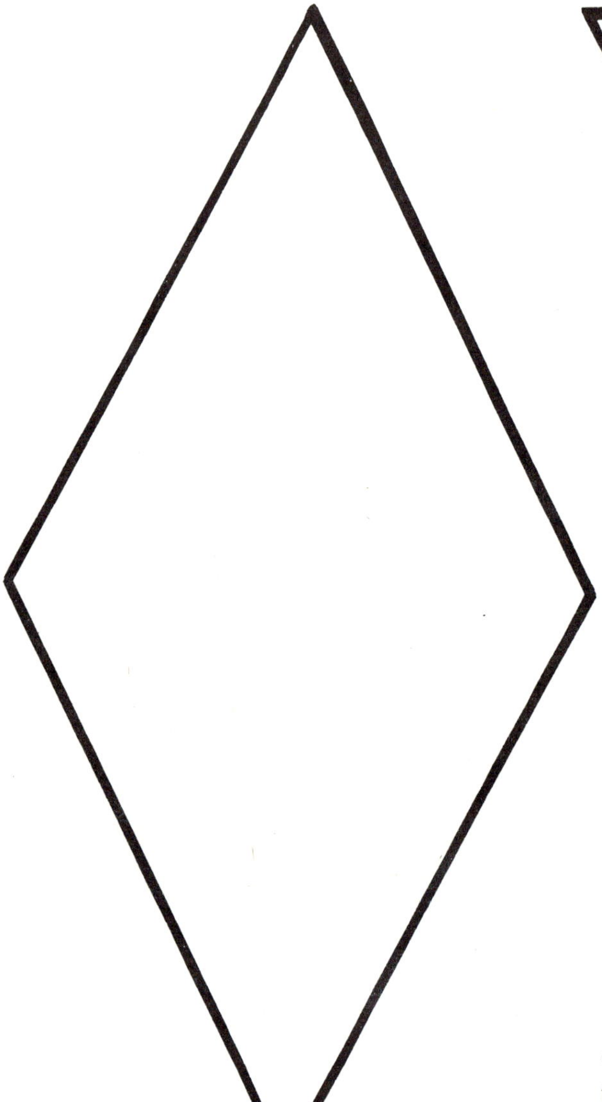

Trace the following diagram and use to make a template. Then cut ten half patches.

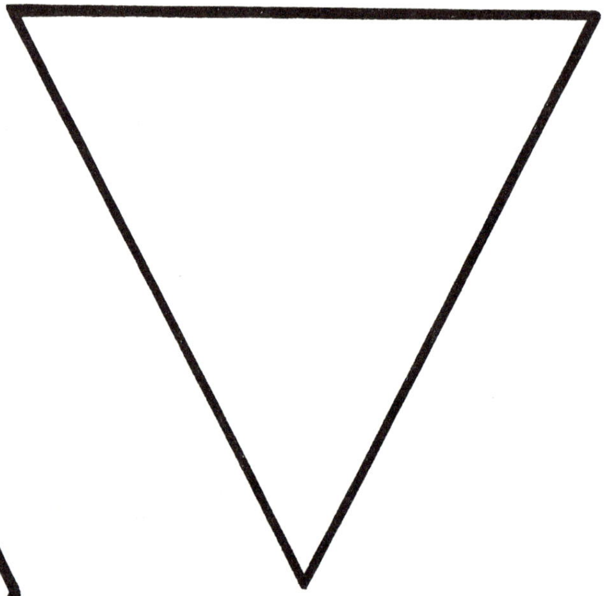

Trace the following diagram and use to make a template. Then cut four vertical half patches.

Making up To make a dark bag with light contrasts. Mount eight whole patches with dark side up, and five whole patches with light side up. Mount ten half patches light side up, and four vertical half patches dark side up.

Arrange patches as shown in the above diagram and sew together. Remove tacking and backing papers. Press well. Press out remaining raw edges so that patchwork measures 40 × 33 cm (16 × 13 in). Place longest edges together, right sides facing. Stitch sides from fold to point of first whole patch. Make handles into rouleau, dark side as right side.

Using dark side as right side throughout and following the above diagram, pin ends of handles 8 cm (3 in) from ends of top part of bag and sew firmly into place. Put second piece over top and work 1.5 cm ($\frac{5}{8}$ in) flat seam along both short edges and top long edge. Trim off corners and turn right side out. Press. Gather edge of patchwork to fit top part, leaving 1.5 cm ($\frac{5}{8}$ in) extending each side. Work 1.5 cm ($\frac{5}{8}$ in) flat seam through all three layers. Attach handles and top of bag to other edge of patchwork in the same way.

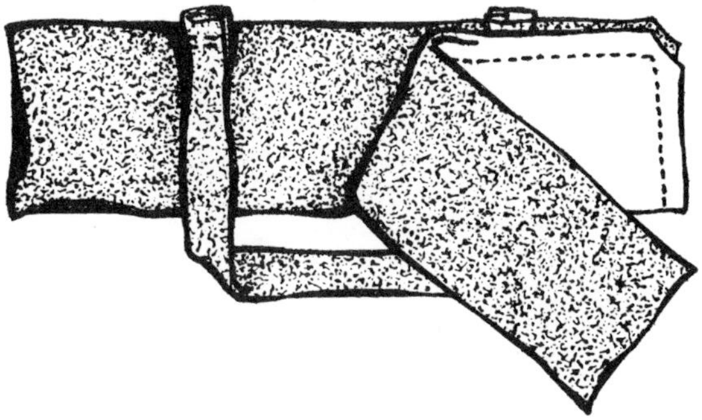

Place longest edges of lining together and stitch sides from fold for 8 cm (3 in). For a dark lining put dark sides together – very practical. Or put light sides together for a light lining. Turn 1.5 cm ($\frac{5}{8}$ in) to wrong side on all remaining edges. Put lining inside bag. Oversew side openings. Gather top edge of lining and sew to cover raw edges. Push bottom corners of bag inwards.

For a dark bag with light contrasts mount patches the other way up, i.e. for light side read dark side, and vice versa. Use light side as right side for handles and top of bag.

APPLIQUÉ

It is difficult to say where patchwork, the joining of patches, finishes and appliqué, the sewing on of patches, begins. The two techniques are very similar. Appliqué can be used to decorate most of the articles in this book and many ready-made garments, but be sure to shrink the denim you use for the patches. It can also be used to cover torn knees, worn elbows and other signs of wear and tear, particularly on children's clothes. There are several methods of appliqué, each suited to a particular type of design, or a particular worker. Try them on spare fabric and find out which suits you best.

First method

This method is only suitable for simple shapes unless you are nimble fingered – because the denim can fray and stretch as you fold turnings.

Equipment Basic sewing equipment; tracing paper; carbon paper.

Technique Trace design and enlarge to correct size. Transfer to wrong side of denim.

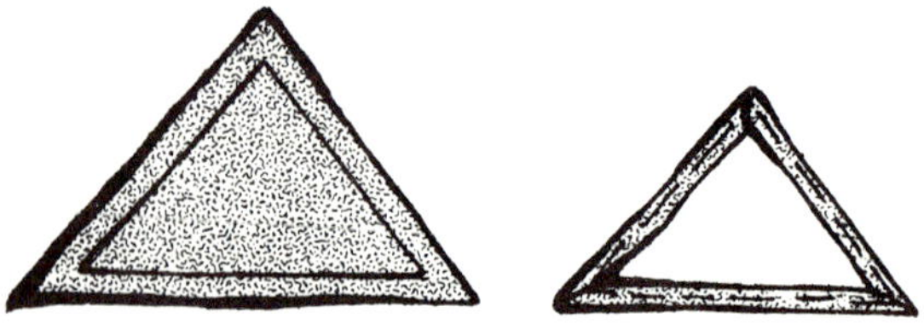

a) Cut out, leaving 1.5 cm ($\frac{5}{8}$ in) all round for turnings.
b) Turn this margin to wrong side of patch and tack in place. Take especial care over corners, folding them as for hand patchwork.

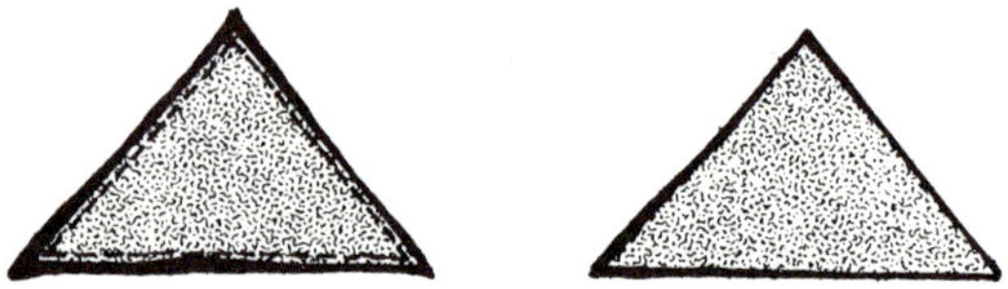

c) Position patch on article and topstitch or hem into place.
d) Remove tacking and press.

Second method
This is very similar to patchwork, by backing the fabric you make it easier to handle and can use more complex shapes – but you must use washable material for the backing shapes as they cannot be removed.
Equipment Basic sewing equipment; tracing paper; carbon paper; interlining.

Technique Trace design and enlarge to correct size. Transfer to interlining and cut out carefully – on the line. Pin interlining to wrong side of denim and cut out, leaving 1.5 m ($\frac{5}{8}$ in) all round for turnings. Tack edge of interlining to denim. Make sure that the fabrics lie flat. (If you use an iron-on interlining you can bond the fabrics together.) Continue as for first method.

Third method
This method is suitable for all designs. If you are lucky enough to have a swing needle machine it is the quickest. Since all the edges of the patch are covered there is no need for turnings. Contrast embroidery will add interest to a very simple design.
Equipment Basic sewing equipment; tracing paper; carbon paper; iron-on interlining; thread for embroidery.
Technique Trace design and enlarge to correct size.

Transfer design to the dull side of the interlining. (The shiny, slightly rough side, has glue on it.) Cut interlining to approximate size and bond to wrong side of denim. Cut out on line. (The interfacing stops the fabric fraying whilst it is embroidered into place.) Position motif on article and tack into place, close to edge. Use close blanket stitch or machine satin stitch to embroider into place.

Fourth method
The quilted effect of this method gives added surface interest and detail. You cannot use interlining to stop the edges fraying as it makes the denim too stiff and unyielding, but the results are worth the extra time and trouble.
Equipment Basic sewing equipment; tracing paper; carbon paper; washable quilting fabric; thread for embroidery.
Technique Trace design and enlarge to correct size.

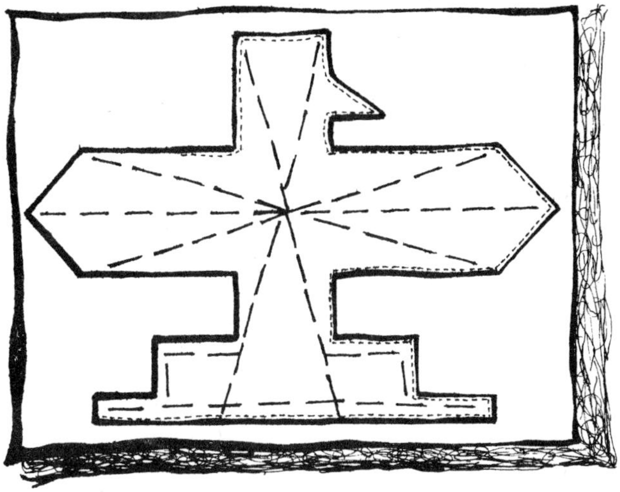

Transfer to right side of denim. Cut quilting fabric to approximate size and tack to wrong side of denim. Use large stitches and tack from centre to keep layers flat. Then using machine stitching or small back stitch, sew just inside design line. With small, very sharp scissors cut as close to stitching as possible – without cutting the thread. Position motif on article and use close blanket stitch or machine satin stitch to embroider it into place. Extra detail can be added by further embroidery through all three layers of fabric.

Jacket in three sizes

An edge to edge jacket in three sizes with very simple appliqué.

Large
To fit 95–105 cm (38–42 in) chest, length 75 cm (30 in), sleeve seam 45 cm (18 in).
Materials 2.9 m ($3\frac{1}{4}$ yd) medium or heavyweight denim – which should be at least 2.6 m ($2\frac{7}{8}$ yd) after shrinking; thread to match; hook and eye or other fastening; depending on chosen method of appliqué: thread for embroidery, 25 cm ($\frac{1}{4}$ yd) interlining, 25 cm ($\frac{1}{4}$ yd) washable quilting fabric.
Cutting out Wash and press denim. Then following the diagram below cut denim across width to give 70 × 90 cm (27 × 36 in) for back, and two pieces, each 40 × 90 cm (16 × 36 in) for fronts.

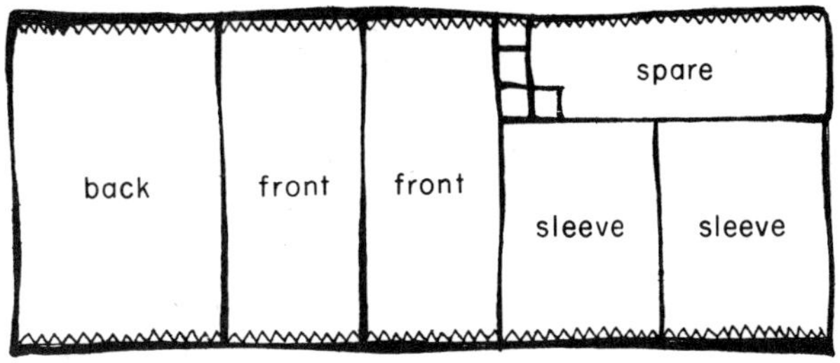

From selvedge of remaining fabric cut a 30 cm (12 in) strip. This fabric is used for appliqué and gussets. Cut remaining fabric in half to give two pieces, each 60 × 55 cm (24 × 22 in) for sleeves. From spare fabric cut four 10 cm (4 in) squares for gussets.

Making up To make a dark jacket with light borders and appliqué, use dark side as right side. For a light jacket with dark borders and appliqué, use light side as right side.

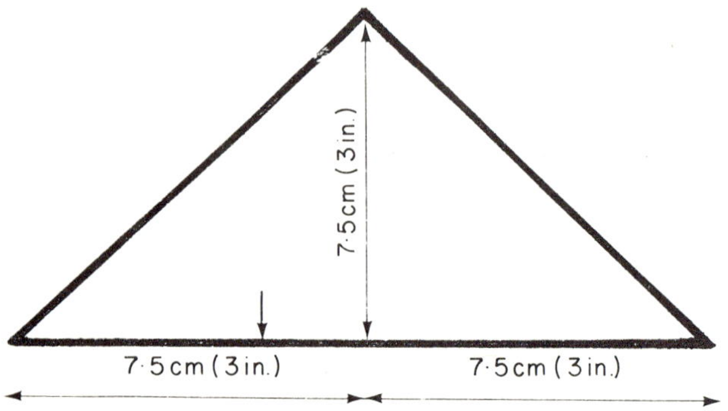

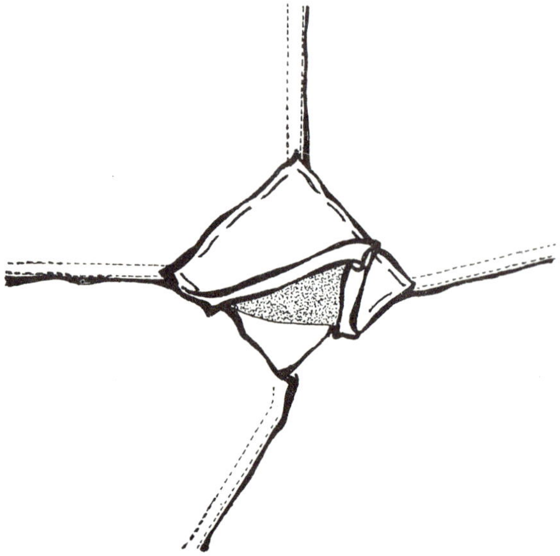

Following the above diagram, make template for appliqué. Then, following instructions for chosen method of appliqué, prepare fourteen triangular patches, remembering to use the reverse side of the denim. On one front mark 5 cm (2 in) margin on long side (this is front edge), and a 25 cm (10 in) margin on short side (bottom edge). Position and tack one triangle with its short edges against the lines forming the corner. Place three more triangles with their long, 15 cm (6 in) edges on front line and one triangle with its long edge on bottom line. Tack and stitch triangles into place. Complete second front to match, making sure that you have a left and a right front. On right side of back mark 25 cm (10 in) margin on one short side (bottom edge). Position four triangles with their 15 cm (6 in) edge on this line. Tack and stitch into place.

With wrong sides together, place fronts on top of back, making sure that the front edges are the correct way round. Match top edges (fronts will overlap a little). Work 2.5 cm (1 in) flat seam across shoulder, leaving 30 cm (12 in) unstitched at centre for neck opening. Press seam open. Turn and stitch 1.5 cm ($\frac{5}{8}$ in) hems along entire length of shoulder, neck and front edges. Place centre of shorter edge of sleeve to shoulder seam. Work run and fell seam. Join sleeve and side edges using run and fell seams. Leave 7.5 cm (3 in) unstitched at underarm.

Turn in and tack 1.5 cm ($\frac{5}{8}$ in) on all edges of gussets. Then following the diagram below stitch into place at underarm, one on the inside, one on the outside. Hem neatly into place.

Stitch 10 cm (4 in) hems on sleeves and bottom edge. Fold front corners to make revers. Sew on hook and eye; or cut two 5 cm (2 in) strips and make these into rouleaux to use as a tie fastening.

To adjust length If you want to shorten or lengthen this jacket slightly, make the bottom and sleeve hems wider or narrower, but remember to adjust the position of the appliqué or it could be covered by the hems. To make a much shorter jacket cut strip from the short edge of fronts and back, and the long edge of sleeves. You will not have to reposition the appliqué.

Medium

To fit 80–90 cm (32–36 in) chest, length 75 cm (30 in), sleeve seam 45 cm (18 in).

Materials 2.7 m (3 yd) medium or heavyweight denim – which should be at least 2.6 m ($2\frac{7}{8}$ yd) after shrinking; thread to match; hook and eye or other fastening; depending on chosen method of appliqué: thread for embroidery, 25 cm ($\frac{1}{4}$ yd) interlining, 25 cm ($\frac{1}{4}$ yd) washable quilting fabric.

Cutting out Wash and press denim. Then following the diagram for cutting out the large jacket, cut denim across width to give 60 × 90 cm (24 × 36 in) for back, and two pieces each 35 × 90 cm (14 × 36 in) for fronts. From selvedge of remaining fabric cut a 30 cm (12 in) strip. This fabric is used for appliqué and gussets. Cut remaining fabric in half to give two pieces, each 60 × 55 cm (24 × 22 in) for sleeves. From spare fabric cut four 10 cm (4 in) squares for gussets.

Making up Make up as for large jacket but leave 25 cm (10 in) unstitched for neck opening.

Small

To fit 65–75 cm (26–30 in) chest, length 60 cm (24 in), sleeve seam 40 cm (16 in).

Jacket

Materials 1.7 m (2 yd) medium or heavyweight denim – which should be at least 1.5 m ($1\frac{3}{4}$ yd) after shrinking; thread to match; hook and eye or other fastening; depending on chosen method of appliqué: thread for embroidery, 10 cm ($\frac{1}{8}$ yd) interlining, 10 cm ($\frac{1}{8}$ yd) washable quilting fabric.
Cutting out Wash and press denim. Then following the diagram below, cut across width of fabric to give 55 × 90 cm (22 × 36 in). Cut this in half to give two pieces, each 55 × 45 cm (22 × 18 in) for sleeves. From selvedge of remaining fabric cut 15 cm (6 in) strip. This fabric is used for appliqué and gussets. Across width of remaining fabric cut 45 × 75 cm (18 × 30 in) for back and two pieces each 25 × 75 cm (10 × 30 in) for fronts. From spare fabric cut four 10 cm (4 in) squares for gussets.

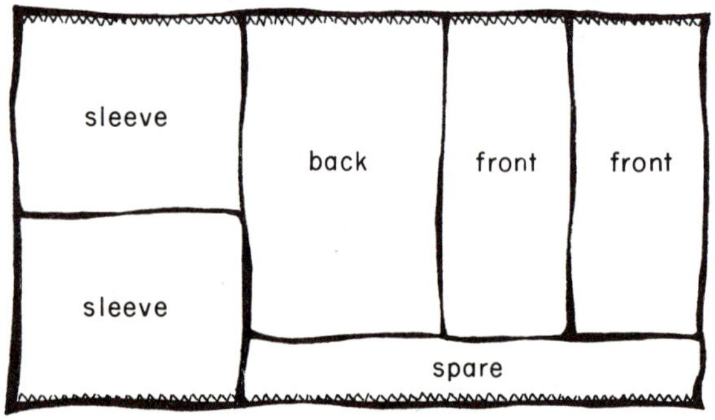

Making up Trace the diagram below and use to make templates for appliqué. Then make up as for large jacket, but leaving 22.5 cm (9 in) unstitched for neck opening.

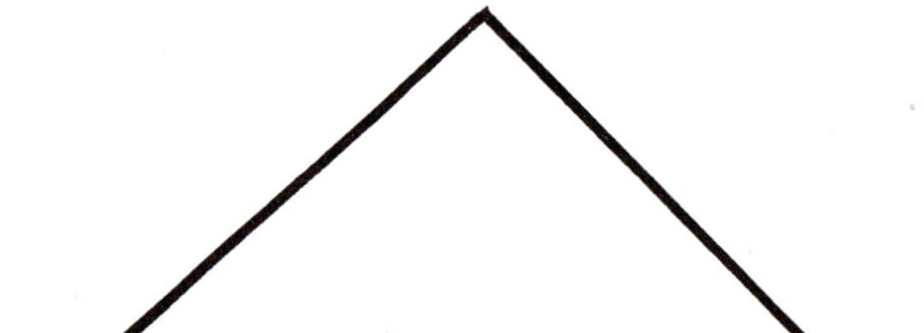

Reversible jacket
If made without appliqué this jacket can be worn dark or light side out – depending on your mood. This basic jacket can also be decorated in other ways. It could easily be painted, printed or embroidered.

Gathered skirt with wrap-over front in two sizes

Large
Calf length skirt with tie fastening to fit 60–70 cm (24–28 in) waist, length 75 cm (30 in).
Materials 2.8 m ($3\frac{1}{8}$ yd) of medium or light-weight denim which should be at least 2.5 m ($2\frac{3}{4}$ yd) after shrinking; thread to match; depending on chosen method of appliqué: thread for embroidery, 20 cm ($\frac{1}{4}$ yd) interlining, 20 cm ($\frac{1}{4}$ yd) washable quilting fabric.
Cutting out Wash and press denim. Then, following the diagram below, cut two 15 cm (6 in) strips across width of fabric for waist band and ties, and 200 cm (80 in) for skirt. This leaves 20 × 90 cm (7 × 36 in) for appliqué.

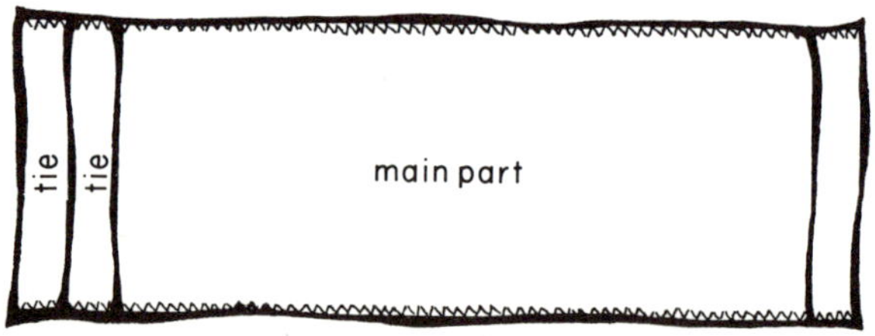

Making up To make a dark skirt with light appliqué and borders, use dark side as right side. For a light skirt with dark appliqué and borders, use light side as right side. This design cannot easily be worked using the first method of appliqué, but any other method is suitable. The stem of the flower needs to be embroidered.

Trace the design below and enlarge to 30 cm (12 in) square. Use this to cut templates for leaf and flower. Prepare two leaf shapes and one flower. (Remember to use reverse side of denim.)

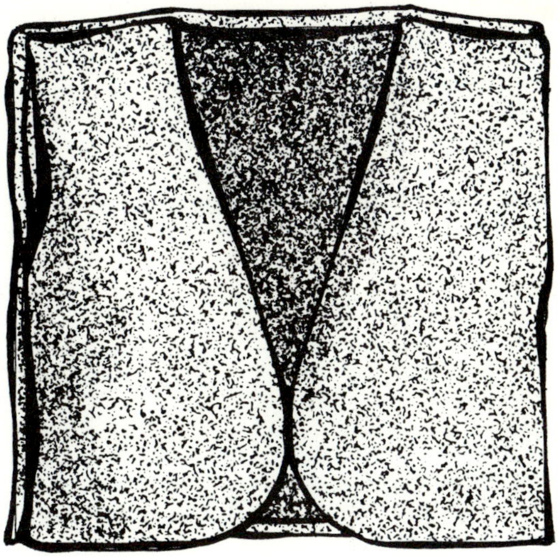

Gathered skirt and jacket

Spread out main part of denim, right side up, and mark 25 cm (10 in) margin on right-hand edge. Mark 25 cm (10 in) margin on bottom edge. (You do not have to mark the entire length, but make sure that it is the right-hand corner or your appliqué will come under the wrap-over.) Mark diagonal line through corner for stalk of flower. Position flower and leaf shapes and sew into position. Embroider stem. Turn and stitch 10 cm (4 in) hems on bottom and side edges. Be sure to mitre the corners.

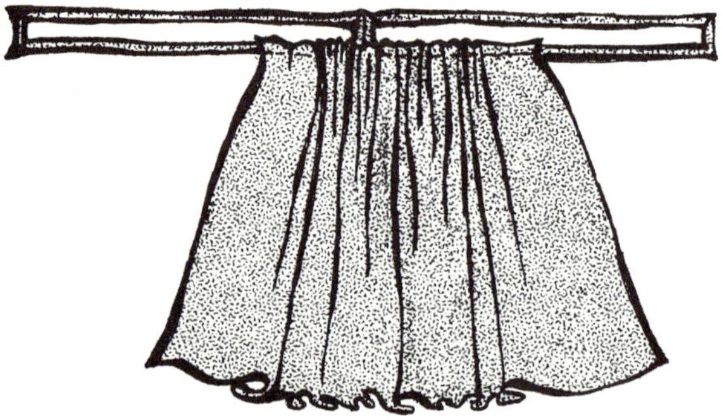

Run gathering thread along top edge. Wrap skirt round you, overlapping 30 cm (12 in) at front. Pull up gathering threads until skirt fits waist – do not gather up over lap. Mark right-hand side of skirt, this is where the slit will be. Join short edges of waistband and ties with a flat seam, wrong sides together. Match seam to right-hand mark on skirt. (The ties will not be the same length.) Seam skirt to band using a 1.5 cm ($\frac{5}{8}$ in) flat seam. Fold 1.5 cm ($\frac{5}{8}$ in) to right side on remaining edges of waistband and ties. Fold band in half and oversew or topstitch edges. Hem remaining edge of band to cover raw edges.

Carefully snip through part of stitching at side seam of band. Oversew edges to form slit.

Small skirt

For a child, to fit 45–55 cm (18–22 in) waist, length 60 cm (24 in).

Materials 2.2 m ($2\frac{3}{8}$ yd) of any weight denim – after shrinking this should be at least 2 m ($2\frac{1}{8}$ yd); thread to match; depending on chosen method of appliqué: thread for embroidery; 20 cm ($\frac{1}{4}$ yd) interlining; 20 cm ($\frac{1}{4}$ yd) washable quilting fabric.

Cutting out Wash and press denim. Then, following the diagram below, cut 15 cm (6 in) strip from selvedge. Cut in half to give two pieces each 15 × 100 cm (6 × 40 in) for waistband and ties. From remaining denim cut 175 × 75 cm (70 × 30 in) for main part of skirt. This leaves 25 × 75 cm (6 × 30 in) for appliqué.

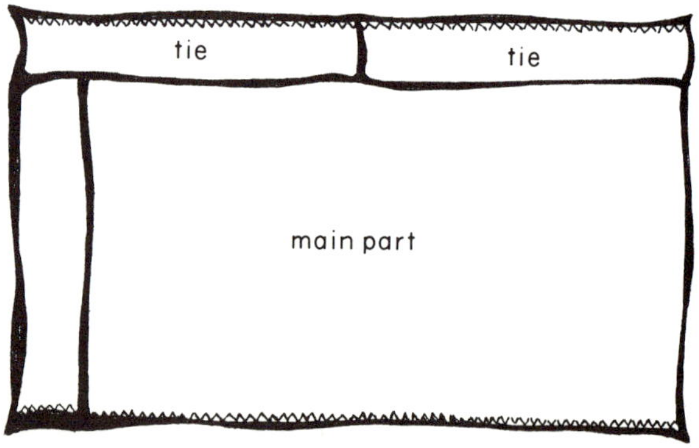

Making up Trace the design given for the gathered skirt, and enlarge to 22.5 cm (9 in) square. Cut templates for leaf and flower. Then make up as for large skirt, but make the overlap 22.5 cm (9 in) instead of 30 cm (12 in).

Back view of jacket

Short jacket in three sizes

To wear with gathered skirt or jeans. It comes in three sizes.

Large
To fit 95–105 cm (38–42 in) chest, length 40 cm (16 in).
Materials 1 m ($1\frac{1}{8}$ yd) of any weight denim – which should be at least 0.9 m (1 yd) after shrinking; thread to match; depending on method of the appliqué: thread for embroidery, 20 cm ($\frac{1}{4}$ yd) interlining, 20 cm ($\frac{1}{4}$ yd) washable quilting fabric.
Cutting out Wash and press denim. Then following the diagram below cut fabric in half lengthways between selvedges to give two pieces, each 90 × 45 cm (36 × 18 in). From one piece cut 70 × 45 cm (27 × 18 in) for back, and leaving 20 × 45 cm (9 × 18 in) for appliqué. From second piece cut two fronts, each 40 × 45 cm (16 × 18 in). Mark 15 cm (6 in) from corner on one short side. From same corner mark 30 cm (12 in) on long edge. Join marks and cut off corner for neck edge. Round off bottom corner. Cut second front to match, making sure that you have a left and right front.

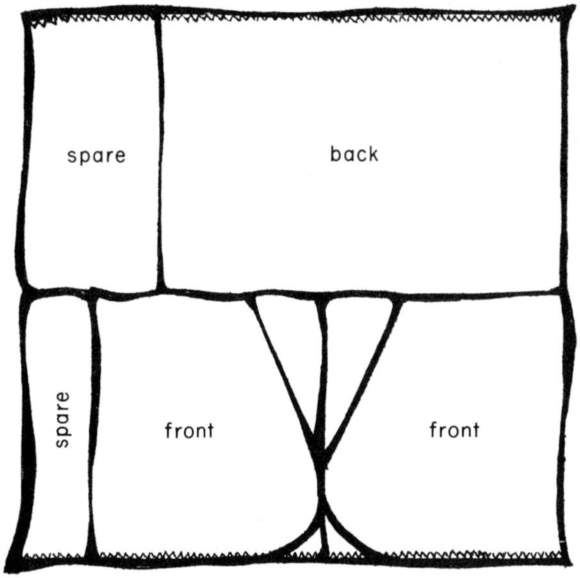

Making up To make a light jacket with dark appliqué, use light side as right side. For a dark jacket with light appliqué, use dark side as right side. This design cannot be easily worked using the first method, but any other method is suitable. The stem of the flower needs to be embroidered. Trace the design given for the gathered skirt and enlarge to 30 cm (12 in) square, and use to cut templates for leaf and flower. Prepare two leaf shapes and one flower, remembering to use reverse side of denim. Mark centres of long edge of back. Join marks and using this line to mark stem arrange patches and stitch into place.

With wrong sides together, join shoulder seams, using 2.5 cm (1 in) flat seams. Press seams open. Make side seams into 1.5 cm ($\frac{5}{8}$ in) hems along their entire length to neaten armholes. Make shoulder seams into 1.5 cm ($\frac{5}{8}$ in) hems. This will neaten the back of the neck. Turn 1.5 cm ($\frac{5}{8}$ in) hems on front and bottom edges. Turn right side out and press.

Medium
To fit 80–90 cm (32–36 in) chest, length 40 cm (16 in).
Materials 0.9 m (1 yd) of any weight denim – after shrinking this should be at least 0.8 m ($\frac{7}{8}$ yd); thread to match; depending on chosen method of appliqué: thread for embroidery, 20 cm ($\frac{1}{4}$ yd) interlining, 20 cm ($\frac{1}{4}$ yd) washable quilting fabric.
Cutting out Wash and press denim. Then, following the diagram for cutting out the large size, cut fabric in half lengthways between selvedges to give two pieces, each 90 × 60 cm (32 × 18 in). From one piece cut 60 × 45 cm (24 × 18 in) for back, leaving 20 × 45 cm (8 × 18 in) for appliqué. From second piece cut two fronts, each 35 × 45 cm (14 × 18 in). Mark 15 cm (6 in) from corner on one short side. From same corner mark 30 cm (12 in) on long side. Join marks and cut off corner for neck edge. Round off bottom corner. Cut second side to match, making sure that you have a left-hand and a right-hand front.
Making up Make up as for large jacket.

Small
For a child. To fit 65–75 cm (26–30 in) chest, length 30 cm (12 in).
Materials 0.6 m ($\frac{5}{8}$ yd) of any weight denim – this should be at least 0.5 m (20 in) after shrinking; thread to match; depending on chosen method of appliqué: thread for embroidery, 20 cm ($\frac{1}{4}$ yd) interlining, 20 cm ($\frac{1}{4}$ yd) washable quilting fabric.

Cutting out Wash and press denim. Then, following the diagram below cut 35 × 90 cm (14 × 36 in), leaving 15 cm (6 in) for appliqué. From first piece cut 35 × 40 cm (14 × 16 in) for back, and two pieces 35 × 22.5 cm (14 × 10 in) for fronts. Mark 10 cm (4 in) from one corner on short side. From same corner mark 20 cm (8 in) on long side. Join marks and cut off corner for neck edge. Round off bottom corners as shown. Cut second front to match, making sure that you have a left and a right front.

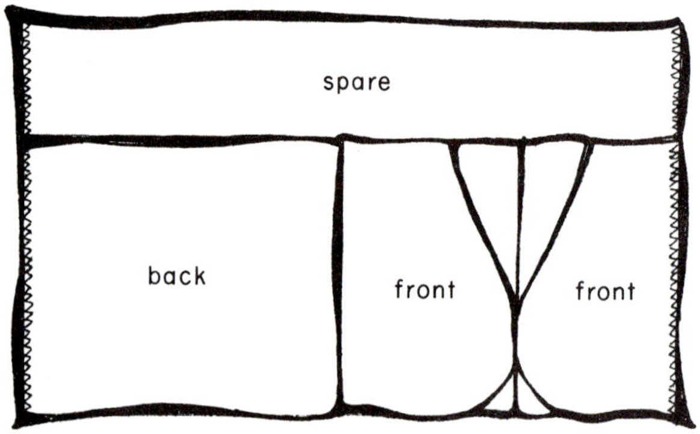

Making up Trace the design given for the gathered skirt and enlarge to 20 cm (8 in) square. Use to cut out templates for leaf and flower. Make up as for large jacket.

Dress in three sizes

Calf length with full length sleeves. The appliqué has embroidered detail and was inspired by the illustrations found in a book on the North American Indians. It comes in three sizes.

Large
To fit 95–105 cm (38–42 in) bust, length 105 cm (42 in), sleeve seam 45 cm (18 in).
Materials 4 m (4⅜ yd) of medium or lightweight denim – after shrinking this should be at least 3.5 m (3⅞ yd); thread to match; depending on chosen method of appliqué: thread for embroidery, 0.5 m (½ yd) interlining, 0.5 m (½ yd) washable quilting fabric.
Cutting out Wash and press denim. Then, following the diagram below cut across width to give two pieces, each 120 × 90 cm (48 × 36 in). From the selvedge of the first piece cut a 20 cm (8 in) strip (for appliqué), leaving 120 × 70 cm (48 × 28 in) for back. From the selvedge of second piece cut a 10 cm (4 in) strip (for appliqué), leaving 120 × 80 cm (48 × 32 in). Cut this piece in half to give two fronts each 120 × 40 cm (48 × 16 in). From selvedge of remaining fabric cut a 30 cm (12 in) strip (for appliqué), leaving 110 × 55 cm (44 × 22 in). Cut this to give two sleeves, each 55 cm (22 in) square. From spare fabric cut four 10 cm (4 in) squares for gussets.

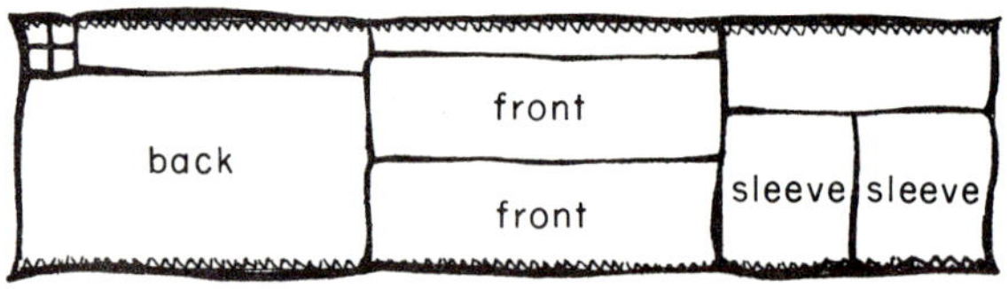

Making up To make a dark dress with light hems and appliqué, use dark side as right side. For a light dress with dark hems and appliqué, use light side as right side.

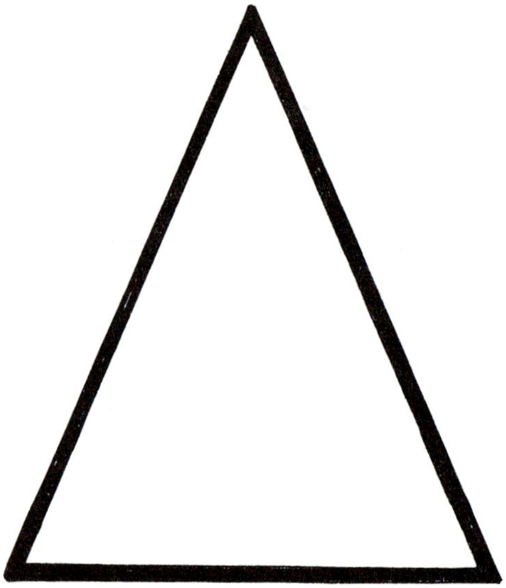

Trace the above diagram and use to make templates for triangles.

Trace the following diagram and enlarge to 20 × 37.5 cm (8 × 15 in). Prepare four bodies and sixteen triangles. Remember to use reverse side of denim. This design is not easily worked using the first method, but any other method is suitable.

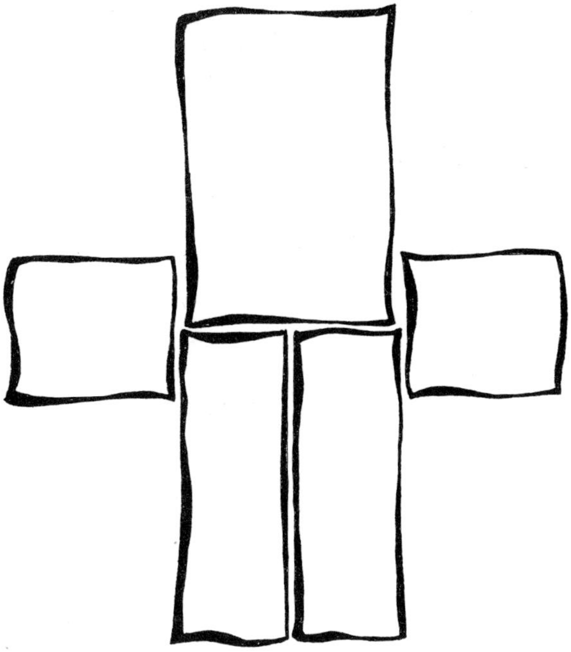

On right side of back, mark 5 cm (2 in) margin on both long edges, and a 25 cm (10 in) margin on one short edge (bottom edge). Mark fronts in the same way. Place appliqué pieces within these margins. Finished design should be about 50 × 30 cm (20 × 12 in). Sew patches into place, embroider eyes and details of head dress. (If using machine satin stitch use a small block of this for the eyes.)

With wrong sides together, match sleeve edges, fronts will overlap. Work 2.5 cm (1 in) flat seam across shoulders, leaving 30 cm (12 in) unstitched at centre for neck opening. Press seam open. Joint fronts, wrong sides together, using a 2.5 cm (1 in) flat seam, wrong sides together. Leave 15 cm (6 in) unstitched at top for front opening.

Press all seams open. Place centre of one edge of sleeve to shoulder seam, wrong sides together. Work 2.5 cm (1 in) flat seam. Join side seams, using 2.5 cm (1 in) flat seams. Leaving 40 cm (16 in) open at bottom for side slit, and 7.5 cm (3 in) open at underarm. Press seams open. Make all seams into 1.5 cm ($\frac{5}{8}$ in) hems. Join underarm seams, using a run and fell seam and leaving 7.5 cm (3 in) unstitched at underarm. Prepare gussets and sew into place at underarm (see diagram on page 72). Turn and stitch 10 cm (4 in) hems on bottom edges of back, front and sleeves.

To adjust length To lengthen or shorten slightly, make the bottom and sleeve hems wider or narrower, but remember to change the position of appliqué – or it could be covered by the hem. The dress can be made considerably shorter – work out how much shorter it is to be, and take twice this amount from the yardage given. In either case be sure to adjust length of back and front as you cut them. You will not have to adjust the position of the appliqué.

Medium

To fit 80–90 cm (32–36 in) bust, length 105 cm (42 in) sleeve seam 45 cm (18 in).

Materials 4 m ($4\frac{3}{8}$ yd) medium or lightweight

Dress

denim – after shrinking this should be at least 3.5 m ($3\frac{7}{8}$ yd); thread to match; depending on chosen method of appliqué: thread for embroidery, 0.5 m ($\frac{1}{2}$ yd) interlining, 0.5 m ($\frac{1}{2}$ yd) washable quilting fabric.

Cutting out Wash and press denim. Then following the diagram for cutting out the large size, cut across width to give two pieces, each 120 × 90 cm (48 × 36 in). From the selvedge of the first piece cut a 30 cm (12 in) strip (for appliqué), leaving 120 × 60 cm (48 × 24 in) for back. From selvedge of second piece, cut a 20 cm (8 in) strip (for appliqué), leaving 120 × 70 cm (48 × 28 in). Cut this piece to give two fronts, each 120 × 35 cm (48 × 14 in). From selvedge of remaining fabric cut a 30 cm (12 in) strip (for appliqué) leaving 55 × 110 cm (22 × 44 in). Cut this to give two sleeves, each 55 cm (22 in) square. From spare fabric cut four 10 cm (4 in) squares for gussets.

Making up Make up as for large dress.

Small

To fit a child, chest 65–75 cm (26–30 in), length 95 cm (38 in) and sleeve seam 40 cm (16 in).

Materials 2.4 m ($2\frac{3}{4}$ yd) of medium or lightweight denim – this should be at least 2.2 m ($2\frac{1}{2}$ yd) after shrinking; thread to match; depending on chosen method of appliqué: thread for embroidery, 0.2 m ($\frac{1}{4}$ yd) interlining, 0.2 m ($\frac{1}{4}$ yd) washable quilting fabric.

Cutting out Wash and press denim. Then, following the diagram below, cut fabric in half across width to give two pieces, each 110 × 90 cm (44 × 36 in). Cut first piece in half to give two pieces, each 110 × 45 cm (44 × 18 in). From other piece, cut two sleeves, each 45 × 55 cm (18 × 22 in). From remaining fabric cut two fronts, each 110 × 25 cm (44 × 10 in) and leaving 110 × 40 cm (44 × 16 in) for appliqué. From spare fabric cut four 10 cm (4 in) squares for gussets.

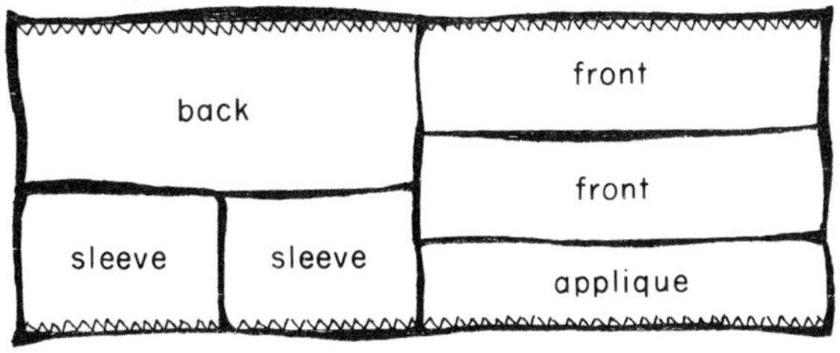

Making up Trace the diagram below and make templates for triangles.

Trace the design for making up the large dress, and enlarge to 16 × 10 cm ($7\frac{1}{2}$ × 4 in). Complete motif will be about 25 × 15 cm (10 × 6 in). Then follow instructions for making up large dress.

Tabard in two sizes and in two lengths

Intended to be worn over jumper or shirt. It comes in two sizes and two lengths.

Calf-length tabard

To fit 85–95 cm (34–38 in) bust, length 110 cm (44 in).

Materials 1.6 m ($1\frac{3}{4}$ yd) heavy or medium weight denim; thread to match; curtain rings; depending on chosen method of appliqué: thread for embroidery, 0.3 m ($\frac{3}{8}$ yd) interlining, 0.3 m ($\frac{3}{8}$ yd) washable quilting fabric.

Cutting out Following the diagram below, cut fabric between selvedges to give two pieces, each 160 × 45 cm (63 × 18 in). From first piece cut 125 × 45 cm (49 × 18 in) for front and seven 5 cm (2 in) strips for ties. From second piece, cut 125 × 45 cm (49 × 18 in) for back and one 5 cm (2 in) strip for remaining tie. This leaves 30 × 45 cm (11 × 18 in) for appliqué.

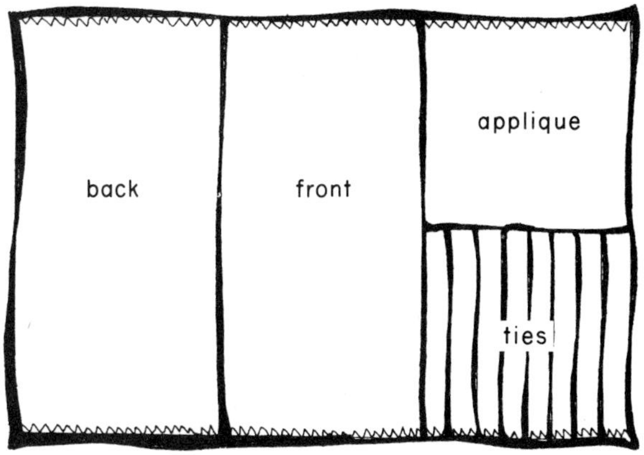

Making up To make a dark tabard with light appliqué and hems, use dark side as right side. For a light tabard with dark appliqué and hems, use light side as right side. On front and back, turn and stitch 1.5 cm ($\frac{5}{8}$ in) hems on one short and both long sides. Make 10 cm (4 in) hem on remaining side (bottom edge).

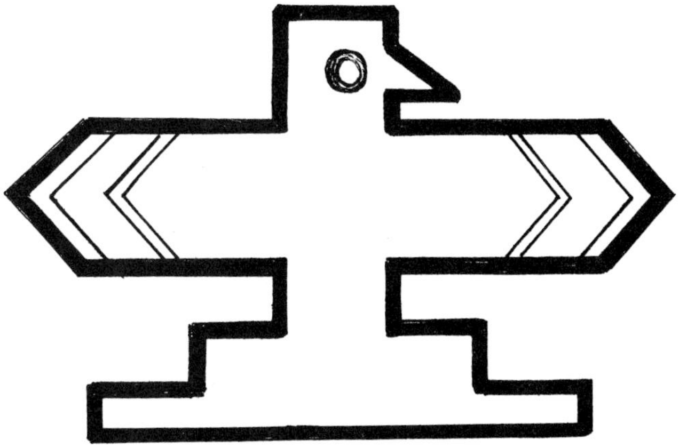

Trace the above diagram and enlarge to 37.5 × 25 cm (15 × 10 in). Prepare motif, remember to use reverse side of denim. Apply to front

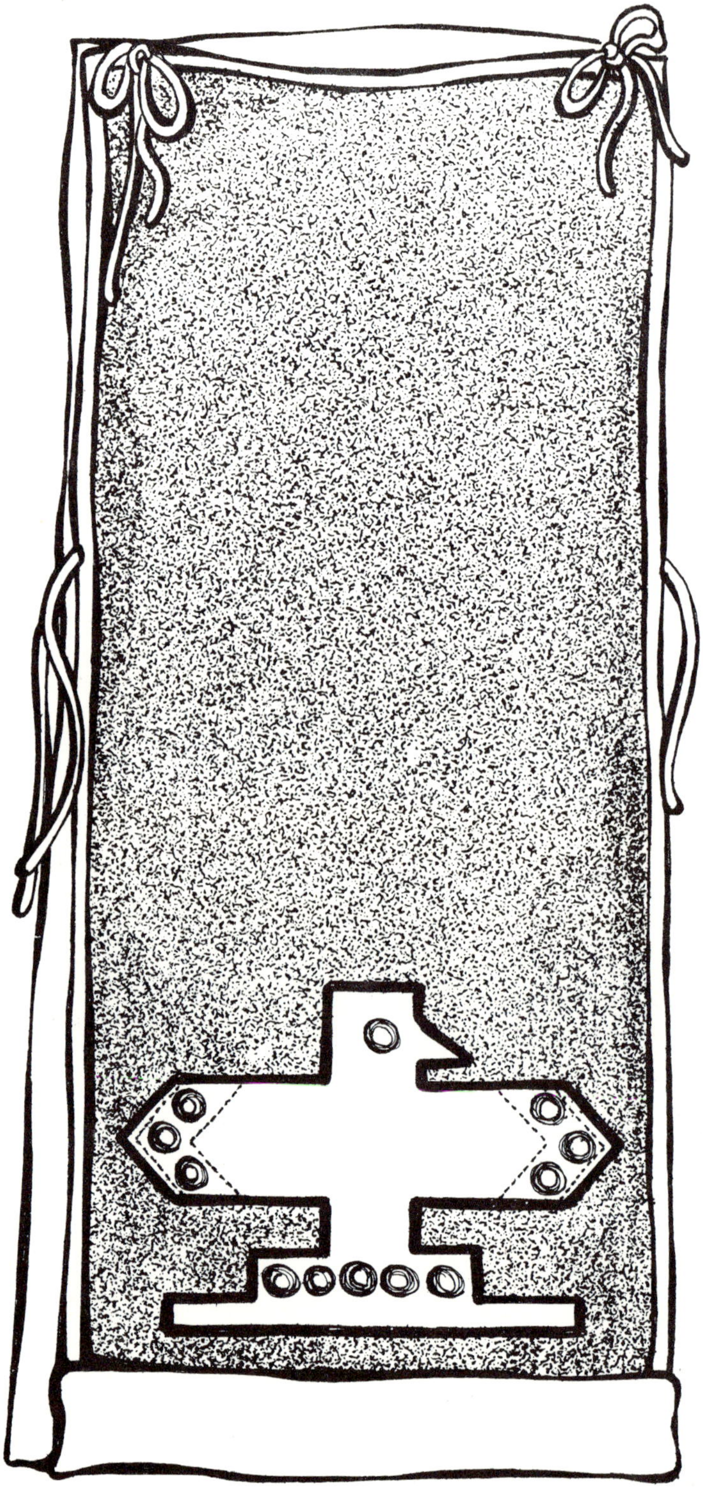

Calf-length tabard

Hip-length tabard

approximately 5 cm (2 in) from upper edge of bottom hem. Embroider wing detail and attach rings. Make ties into rouleaux. Sew one tie to each of four top corners, and other four 35 cm (14 in) down each side hem.

Hip-length tabard
To fit 85–95 cm (34–38 in) bust, length 60 cm (24 in).
Materials 1.1 m (1¼ yd) of heavy or medium-weight denim; thread to match; curtain rings; depending on chosen method of appliqué: thread for embroidery, 0.3 m (⅜ yd) interlining, 0.3 m (⅜ yd) washable quilting fabric.
Cutting out Following the diagram for cutting out the calf length tabard, cut fabric between selvedges to give two pieces, each 110 × 45 cm (45 × 18 in). From the first piece cut 75 × 45 cm (30 × 18 in) for front and seven 5 cm (2 in) strips for ties. From second piece cut 75 × 45 cm (30 × 18 in) for back, and one 5 cm (2 in) strip for remaining tie. This leaves 30 × 45 cm (11 × 18 in) for appliqué.
Making up Make up as for calf length tabard. The illustration shows this smock made up using the motif from the appliquéd dress.

Child's tabard
To fit 65–80 cm (26–32 in) chest, length 75 cm (30 in).
Materials 1.2 m (1⅜ yd) of medium or heavy-weight denim; thread to match; curtain rings; depending on chosen method of appliqué: thread for embroidery, 0.2 m (¼ yd) interlining, 0.2 m (¼ yd) washable quilting fabric.
Cutting out Following the diagram below, across width of fabric cut three pieces, each 40 × 90 cm (16 × 36 in). Keep two for back and front. Cut remaining piece in half to give two pieces each 40 × 45 cm (16 × 18 in). Cut one piece to give eight strips, each 5 × 45 cm (2 × 18 in) for ties. Keep second piece for appliqué.

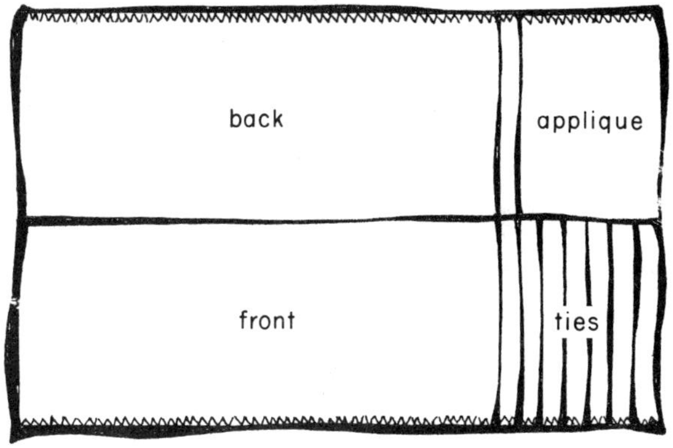

Tabards have come a long way since they were used to identify knights in armour, but they can still be just as individual. The basic tabard could just as easily have the 'indian' appliqué, or simple triangles. To show how easy it is to change the decoration of a basic garment I have illustrated three shawls on the next page.

Decorating basic shawl

Shawl or fichu

Finished size 160 × 75 cm (64 × 30 in).
Materials 1.8 m (2 yd) of any weight denim; thread to match.

The weight of the denim used materially affects the final look of the shawl. Lightweight denim will produce a soft shawl which follows the line of the shoulders – more properly called a fichu, and great to wear in the evenings or as a cover up. Heavy denim produces a stiffer shawl, which tends to stand out from the shoulders and is better worn as an accessory, over a coat perhaps.

Cutting out Following the diagram, right, mark centre of one selvedge of denim and ends of opposite selvedge. Join these marks to produce a triangle. Cut out triangle and keep spare fabric for appliqué.

Making up To make a light shawl with a dark border, use light side as right side. For a dark shawl with a light border, use dark side as right side. On selvedge turn and stitch 1.5 cm ($\frac{5}{8}$ in) hem. On remaining edges turn and stitch 10 cm (4 in) hems. Mitre bottom corner. The upper corners will have to be trimmed and the edge turned under and oversewn into place. Now decorate. You can choose any method described in this book.

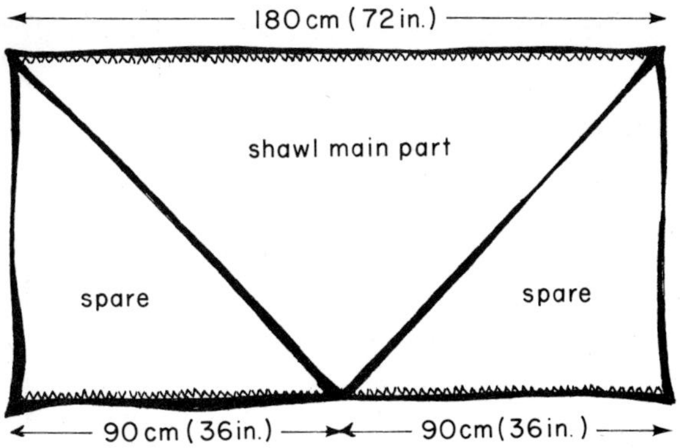

QUILTING

Quilting is one of the oldest forms of embroidery. At first it was purely functional – to add warmth – but today its use is normally decorative, the padding giving relief patterns.

Technique

In quilting a layer of padding is sandwiched between two layers of fabric. Modern quilting fabric is made of manmade fibres, normally terylene, and is washable. It would be impractical to use a non-washable padding with denim – unless you can afford to dry clean the article each time. The fabric flattens slightly as soon as you begin work, so buy a slightly thicker one than you think you need. In the shops it looks deceptively thick, so flatten it between your hands before you decide.

If you are working a complex design such as that on the kimono (see page 91), transfer the design to the right side of the denim using chalk, not carbon. Then sandwich the layer of quilting fabric between the other fabrics and tack all three thicknesses together. This tacking is very important, for the work is spoilt if one layer moves, it looks odd and lumpy. Tack all round the edges first (you can do this by machine) then tack across the fabrics diagonally, both ways. This is firmer than tacking across and down. Make sure that you tack through all three layers.

Stitch along the lines of the design. Use running stitch, stab stitch, back stitch or machine stitch with a matching thread. For a more decorative effect you could use chain stitch and embroidery thread, a machine satin stitch with a contrast thread. Whatever stitch you use make sure that all the stitches go right through all three layers of the quilting.

Single patchwork quilt

Patchwork quilt

This uses both sides of the denim as if they were different fabrics, so you only have to buy two fabrics – not four. It also uses patterned denim, before you buy make sure that it is a woven pattern. Do remember that denim comes in colours other than blue, so this quilt can match the rest of your room. It comes in two sizes and is simply quilted along the lines of the patches.

Single quilt

Approximately 165 × 225 cm (66 × 99 in).

Materials 4 m (4½ yd) patterned denim; 4 m (4½ yd) plain denim (make sure that it is the same weight as the patterned denim); 5.5 m (6¼ yd) of 90 cm (36 in) wide cotton for backing (or you can use an old sheet); 5 m (5⅝ yd) of 90 cm (36 in) wide washable quilting fabric; thread to match.

Cutting out Wash and press denim. Wash and press cotton lining. Cut plain and patterned lining into 18 cm (7 in) squares.

Making up Spread out squares and arrange as shown in the illustration, or in your own pattern. This is easy to do as you only have to turn over squares, not cut extra, if you do not have enough of a particular colour. Starting at one corner, join the first row of eleven squares together. Using a 1.25 cm (½ in) flat seam, right sides together. Press seams open. Join rest of the squares in the same way so that you have fifteen strips. Make sure that these are in the correct order, then join the fifteen strips together using a 1.25 cm (½ in) flat seam, right side to right side. Press all seams open.

Cut quilting fabric in half across width and join long edges together using huge, loose overcasting stitches – be sure that it does not form a ridge. Tack wadding to wrong side of patchwork and trim to same size. Cut lining in half across width and join selvedge edges, right sides together, using a flat seam. Place right side of lining to right side of patchwork. Tack round edges, then trim away any spare lining. Leaving part of one side open so that you can turn the quilt right side out stitch lining to patchwork and quilting 1.25 cm (½ in). from edge. Turn quilt right side out and oversew opening.

Tack layers together, then quilt patchwork by stitching along every seam. If using a machine sew across the width of the quilt and try to keep the bulk of the material to the left of the machine.

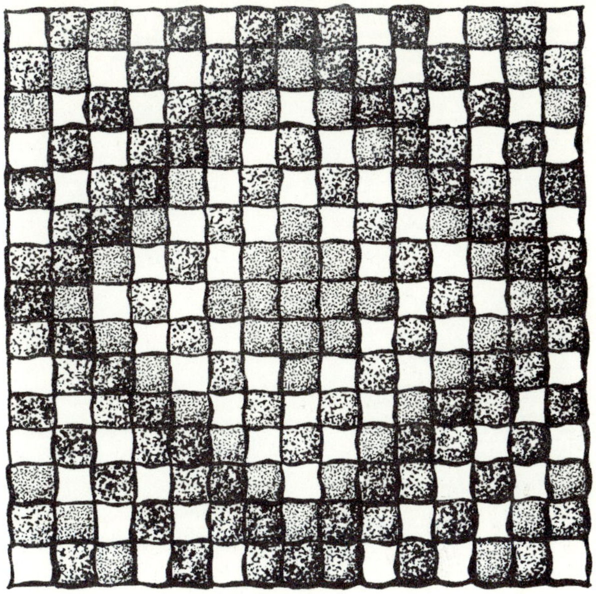

Double patchwork quilt

You can add extra quilting to the centres of some squares if you want.

Double quilt

This will be approximately 225 cm (90 in) square.

Materials 5.2 m (6 yd) of patterned denim; 5.2 m (6 yd) of plain denim (make sure that it is the same weight as the patterned denim); 8.3 m (9 yd) of 90 cm (36 in) wide cotton for backing (or you can use an old sheet); 7.5 m (8½ yd) of 90 cm (36 in) wide washable quilting fabric.

Cutting out Cut out as for single quilt.

Making up Make up as for single quilt, but you will have fifteen squares in each row instead of eleven. Cut lining and quilting fabric into three equal lengths.

MULTI-TECHNIQUE

Now to show off your newly acquired skills.

Kimono

A traditional Japanese garment, made in the traditional way from rectangles. The dragon is a common motif in Japanese art; here, however, a phoenix (the symbol of happiness in Chinese mythology) was chosen to decorate this kimono. To fit 80–95 cm (32–38 in) bust, length 145 cm (58 in).

Materials 8.5 m ($9\frac{1}{2}$ yd) of mediumweight denim – after shrinking this should be at least 7.50 m ($8\frac{3}{8}$ yd); 5.1 m ($5\frac{5}{8}$ yd) of cotton lining 90 cm (36 in) wide – after shrinking this should be at least 4.5 m (5 yd); 1.7 m (2 yd) of cotton fabric 90 cm (36 in) wide – after shrinking this should be at least 1.5 m ($1\frac{3}{4}$ yd) (this is for interlining the sleeve and can be a remnant of patterned fabric, or any spare fabric. It will be completely enclosed in the finished garment); 3.2 m ($3\frac{5}{8}$ yd) of washable quilting fabric; thread to match light side of denim; thread to match dark side of denim; thread for embroidery; curtain rings.

Cutting out Wash and press denim, lining and cotton interlining. Then cut denim into five 150 cm (60 in) lengths.

Then following the diagram below, from the first piece cut two fronts, each 45 × 150 cm (18 × 60 in). From one corner, mark 20 cm (8 in) on the short edge. From the same corner mark 50 cm (20 in) down long edge. Join these points and cut off point for neck. Cut second front to match – make sure that you have a left and right front.

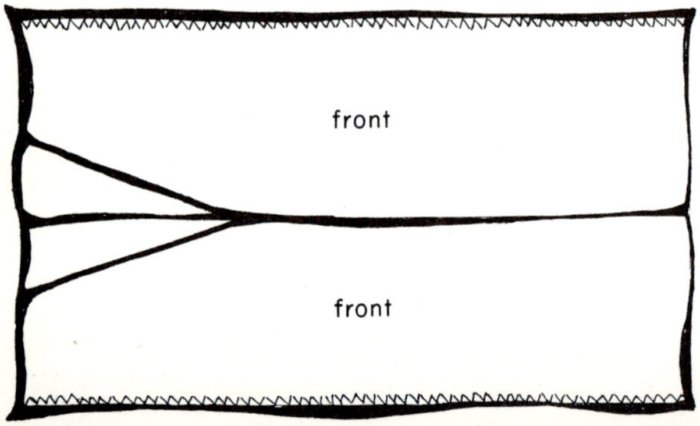

Following the diagram below, from the second piece cut two sleeves, each 40 × 150 cm (16 × 60 in), and one band 10 cm (4 in) wide.

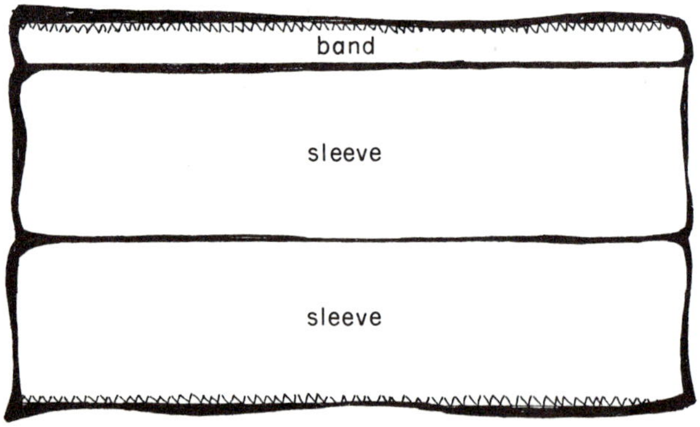

Following the diagram below, from the third rectangle cut 70 × 150 cm (28 × 60 in) for back and two 10 cm (4 in) bands.

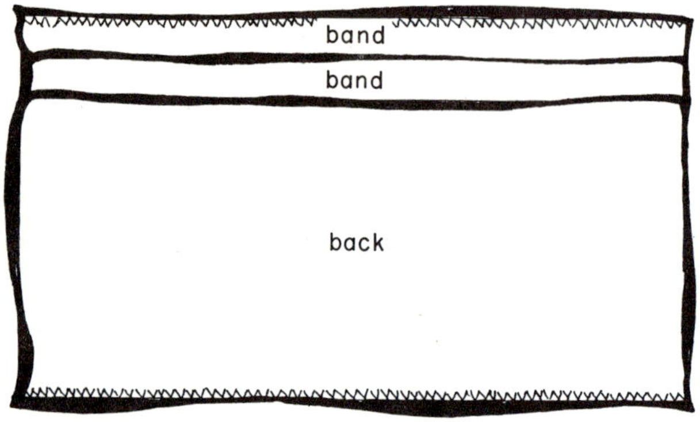

Following the diagram below, from the fourth piece cut three 10 cm (4 in) bands, and one 20 cm (8 in) strip for neck band. This leaves a band 40 × 150 cm (16 × 60 in) for quilting.

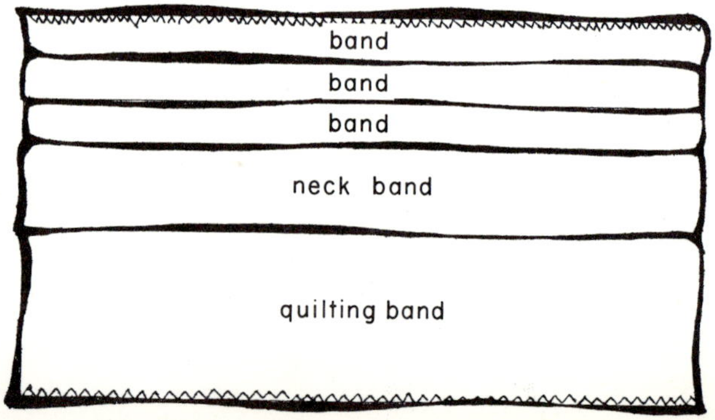

Kimono

Following the diagram below, across width of fifth piece cut two 30 cm (12 in) strips for belt, and two 10 cm (4 in) strips for front bands. The remaining piece is used for appliqué.

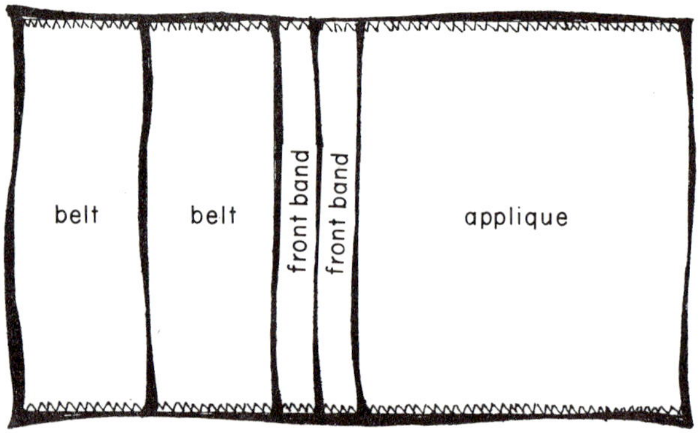

Using denim pieces as patterns, cut one back, two fronts and two sleeves from lining. Then cut two sleeves from cotton interlining. Then following the diagram below, cut two 10 cm (4 in) strips across width of quilting fabric.

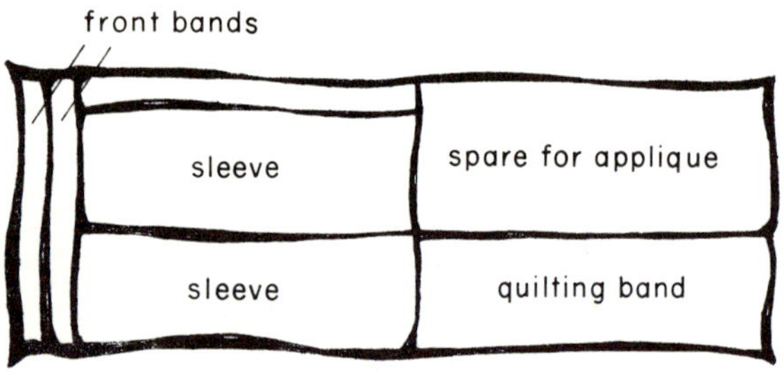

Then cut fabric into two 150 cm (60 in) lengths. From first piece cut two sleeves, each 40 × 150 cm (16 × 60 in). From second piece cut one bottom band 40 × 150 cm (16 × 60 in). Keep spare fabric to pad appliqué.

Making up Trace the design on page 91 and enlarge to 50 cm (20 in) square. Transfer to dark side of spare piece of denim. Using spare quilting fabric and following instructions for padded appliqué tack motif in place 40 cm (16 in) from top edge, and 60 cm (20 in) from bottom edge, on light side of back. Complete embroidery. Quilt wings and body, then add curtain rings where shown. With light side uppermost, work out which is to be the right front. Then mark 50 cm (20 in) margin on bottom edge, and 10 cm (4 in) margins on side edges.

Trace the design below and enlarge to 35 × 30 cm (14 × 12 in). Transfer entire design to front within margins. Transfer leaves only to dark side of spare denim. Pad this shape and appliqué in place. Embroider stems and attach curtain rings.

Using a 1.5 cm ($\frac{5}{8}$ in) flat seam, light sides together sew side seams leaving 35 cm (14 in) unstitched at top for armhole. Press seams open. Trace the design below and enlarge to 40 × 70 cm (16 × 28 in). Transfer to dark side of band for quilting, repeat as necessary.

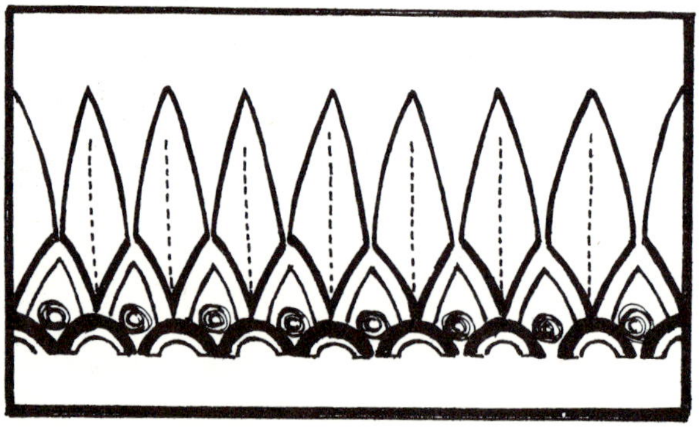

Place one 10 cm (4 in) band, light side up so that its bottom edge is 38.5 cm (15$\frac{3}{8}$ in) from bottom edge of joined fronts and back. Stitch 1.5 cm

($\frac{5}{8}$ in) from bottom edge of band. (This band will fold down to cover the raw edges of the quilting band.) Place quilting fabric then quilting band, matching centres. Tack in place, then quilt. Turn 1.5 cm ($\frac{5}{8}$ in) to wrong side of top band, fold over quilting and hem into place.

Sew shoulder seams. Press. Sew side and shoulder seams of lining, leaving 35 cm (14 in) unstitched for armholes. Pin lining inside denim, wrong side of lining to dark side of denim. Tack round neck and front and bottom edges.

Match centre of neck band to centre of back of neck opening, dark side of band to light side of back. Sew, using 1.5 cm ($\frac{5}{8}$ in) flat seam. Trim off excess length, leaving 1.5 cm ($\frac{5}{8}$ in) for turnings. Turn 1.5 cm ($\frac{5}{8}$ in) to light side on

Back view of kimono

remaining edges of band. Fold band in half. Oversew ends and hem long edge to cover raw edges of neck opening and lining.

Sew on front bands (remember these are the two shorter bands), dark side of band to lining. Stitch using 1.5 cm ($\frac{5}{8}$ in) flat seam. Turn 1.5 cm ($\frac{5}{8}$ in) to light side on remaining edges. Fold band so that it covers raw edges of denim and lining. Hem into place. On one long band, turn 1.5 cm ($\frac{5}{8}$ in) to light side and embroider close to folded edge. Sew other edge of band to bottom edge in the same way that you attached front bands.

Trace the design, right, and enlarge to 40 × 150 cm (16 × 60 in).

Transfer to dark side of sleeve pieces. Tack together denim, quilting fabric and interlining. Quilt as shown. Seam narrow edges of denim only. Overlap quilting fabric and tack in place. Trim down bulk at join if necessary. Overlap edges of interlining, turn under one edge and hem into place. Fold sleeve in half and mark shoulder opposite seam on inside edge. Join short edges of sleeve lining. Place inside quilted sleeve, wrong side next to interlining. Tack round edges, leaving 25 cm (10 in) unstitched at either side of shoulder point. Seam short edges of band, dark sides together, using a 1.5 cm ($\frac{5}{8}$ in) flat seam. Attach to outside edge of sleeve.

Join short edges of second band and embroider as for bottom band. Attach to inside edge of sleeve, leaving 60 cm (20 in) unstitched as for lining. Do not hem into place.

To attach sleeve, snip down to stitching either side of opening. Turn band to front and hem into place. Seam sleeve to body between notches. Light side of body to dark side of sleeve and band. Leave lining loose. Turn garment inside out, fold 1.5 cm ($\frac{5}{8}$ in) to wrong side on lining and hem into place so that it encloses the raw edges of sleeve and body. Make up and attach second sleeve in the same way.

Put on kimono and mark waist. Unpick stitching at waist for 10 cm (4 in) and oversew lining and denim to form slit for belt. Join short edges of belt, using 1.5 cm ($\frac{5}{8}$ in) flat seam, dark sides together. Press. Make up as for rouleaux. Press.

Give garment final press, and thread belt through slits so that it is next to the lining of the back and emerges through the slits. It will then hold the front closed but allow the back to fall free and show off the embroidery, quilting and appliqué to its best advantage.

INDEX

References in italic type denote page numbers of illustrations.